# FOOD, SHELTER
# AND THE
# AMERICAN
# DREAM

## Stanley Aronowitz

A Continuum Book
THE SEABURY PRESS/NEW YORK

FOR CAROL

The Seabury Press
815 Second Avenue
New York, N.Y. 10017

Copyright © 1974 by Stanley Aronowitz

Editor: Michael Roloff
Designed by s. s. DRATE
Printed in the United States of America

LIBRARY OF CONGRESS CATALOGING IN PUBLICATION DATA

Aronowitz, Stanley.
    Food, Shelter, and the American dream.

    (A Continuum book)
    Bibliography:
        1.  United States—Economic conditions—1961–
2.  Energy policy—United States.  3.  Food supply—
United States.  I.  Title.
HC106.6.A7        330.9'73'0924        73–17872
ISBN 0–8164–9192–5

# Contents

# Preface

This book attempts to analyze the forces underlying the food and energy crises that suddenly became the major international events of the past two years. But the subject matter of the book is not confined to the details of the twin crises. Instead, it focuses on the economic, political and social consequences of the elevation of these resources—food and energy—to the major instruments of United States foreign and domestic policy.

Despite the mass of detail pouring almost daily from the press, radio, television and other media, the connections between food and energy remain largely obscure. In fact, it may be said that the more excruciating the specificity of the information supplied, the less we understand about what has been happening and what is likely to happen. The chief reason for this paradox is the lack of historical perspective on the part of the news media. The purpose of this book is to suggest some relationships between the twin crises and the overall shape of economic and social changes within the United States and between this country and the rest of the world.

STANLEY ARONOWITZ

August, 1974

# 1
# Contours of a Troubled Society

At the height of the cold war, Herman Kahn at Hudson Institute urged Americans to begin to "think about the unthinkable." By "unthinkable" Kahn meant the actual possibility that the imperatives of foreign policy might dictate the use, by the United States as well as its adversaries, of nuclear weapons. Kahn was asking us to think in new ways—to give up our taking-for-granted assumptions about the life cycle. The prospect of nuclear warfare had cast a pall over all social relations since the dropping of the first atomic bomb in 1945 on two little-known cities of Japan. Yet, Kahn's invocation to bring the uneasy feeling we all share to the surface of our consciousness was met, quite properly, with outrage and rejection by most Americans.

Thinking about the unthinkable again became the subject of popular discussion in 1973. Throughout the year, government spokesmen, corporation ad men and learned

1

economists spent a good deal of energy reminding us that the old assumptions about the "American Standard of Living" might require scrapping. We were no longer able to take for granted plentiful supplies of relatively cheap food and fuel. In the spring, reports that cattle raisers were holding back beef from the market created a mild panic. Having failed to raise the price of beef some months earlier, food growers and processors were claiming that the supply had dwindled owing to higher costs of production, particularly in such commodities as cattle feed, machinery and fertilizer. Some food shortages did appear. It was hard to find raisins for a while, especially when government price controls were in effect. Even Fig Newtons were not available in all stores. Some cuts of beef were nowhere to be found and we became frightened of a black market in food. By July, controls were lifted on all products except beef, but the government gave us assurances that these controls would expire later in the summer. Miraculously, all shortages did seem to expire with the end of price curbs. Supermarket counters, never bare, were filled to the brim once more. And talk of food scarcity subsided in favor of the "energy crisis."

Slowly we began to realize that *crisis*, a word once reserved for depressions and wars, had now become a household expression. The "Watergate Crisis" was only a warm-up for a much graver condition: everyday life faced profound disruption. Electricity was now said to be in such short supply that "brown-outs" (temporary failure in municipal lighting systems) were an increasing probability. Utility companies were ordered to reduce their output in the midst of summer heat when air conditioners were likely to overload the circuits.

Moreover, the major means of transportation, automobile travel and over-the-road trucking, would have to be restricted because of dwindling quantities of gasoline and diesel fuel. And our furnaces might lack sufficient heating oil. Later in the year, news of paper shortages sent shivers down the collective spines of publishers. Even toilet tissue was in short supply in the California Bay area for a time. The paper shortage was said to be the result of impractical government conservation measures that restricted the right of lumber companies to cut trees and use the timber for paper manufacturing. The price of paper and paper products rose rapidly in fall 1973. For a time, newspapers cut the size of daily editions because of a shortage of newsprint. The price of books rose about 20 percent over the previous year. Book buyers complained that the price of a new paperback was about the same as that of a hardcover edition a few years earlier.

Decorations were not lighted in some shopping areas during the Christmas holidays. The holiday atmosphere was not quite so serious as wartime Great Britain, but the ambience bore some resemblance to that heroic time. President Richard M. Nixon set an example to all Americans by using a commercial airliner to travel to his vacation home rather than the usual "gas guzzling" Presidential jet, so one newspaper reported.

The key word of the year was "shortage." On Saturday, December 29, 1973, *The New York Times* reported oil tankers clogging the New York Harbor while waiting to unload their cargo. It seemed there was a shortage of dock space and storage facilities. That these shortages in storage space may have belied the solemn assurances by government officials that oil was actually in short supply and not being deliberately withheld was not even suggested by the *Times*. Ironically, what the story neglected to mention was that shortages in storage as well as dock facilities may have been a sign of surfeit rather than of depletion. Yet the logic of the *Times* was that surpluses may create shortages of a different kind. Unwittingly, the *Times* perpetuated the deprivation psychology.

Material deprivation has been as remote from the everyday lives of most Americans, and repressed even from their consciousness, as nuclear warfare—at least since the end of the Second World War. Despite the persistence of severe economic straits for at least thirty-five million people, even in the best of times, the majority of workers, blue-collar as well as white-collar, have lived in a culture of plenty. Of course, there have been substantial variations in the living conditions of professionals, technicians and skilled workers, not to mention the majority of workers in industrial and service sectors who have never quite escaped from the shadows of unemployment, temporary shortages of cash and credit, and the harrowing fear that accident or sickness will wipe out their savings and plunge them to the level of the genuinely poor. At different times, even the engineers and scientists have suffered severe depression, especially in periods of transition between the production of certain materials and others. Whole regions have been left destitute by industrial relocation even as the gross national product, that melodic index of "real prosperity," soared to the anthems of government economists.

Yet it is undeniable that for most years since the end of the Second World War, it has not been hard for most workers to find a job even if it wasn't always easy to keep. (Of course, it is often necessary to uproot yourself and your family to find employment.) When cash has run out, bank and other types of credit have been available to purchase cars, homes, appliances or vacations. The dream of a factory worker's child escaping the plant and getting a job in more pleasant surroundings via the route of higher education has been realized in enough instances to make what was once a myth into a realistic expectation for many.

Institutional structures remain dense to human consciousness during times of "normalcy." Perhaps the only benefit of a crisis is that the institutions become transparent, that their structure and power relations are visible to the naked eye. The shroud of secrecy and obscurity within which most corporations operate is temporarily lifted so that a peek into their actual operations can be obtained. Once the crisis is overcome or becomes a routine feature of economic life, such as happened with the food crisis, the secrets are locked up once more. The corporations resume their semi-anonymous existence and price movements once more appear functions of the market mechanisms rather than the deliberate actions of powerful individuals and interests.

The extractive industries, specifically food, cotton, lumber and "energy" resources such as coal, oil and natural gas, still form the foundation of our economic life as well as our material culture: the important new insight generated by the various shortages with which Americans were confronted in 1973 is that rising on the foundation of relatively cheap food and energy are the complex of manufacturing industries and services that constitute the so-called "infrastructure" of the economy. There can be no rails, trucks, air travel without oil, and no communications can function without coal-fueled electricity. The giant chemical industry, of which plastics is an important branch, is largely dependent on oil. Most passenger transportation is provided by the automobile, often considered the key industry in the nation because it consumes huge quantities of steel, plastics, and rubber as well as oil. In 1950, oil accounted for 45 percent of all energy resources. By 1970 it comprised 70 percent of our energy resources. The ability of the United States to dominate the world is attributable in large measure to such fortuitous factors as cheap food made possible by rich, arable land and plentiful supplies of coal and oil within its borders.

Even though other important minerals, including large quantities of oil, have been extracted from other areas of the world, the United States itself has always accounted for the lion's share of technical preconditions of its own industrial development. The Middle East has been virtually insignificant in terms of United States industrial growth. Rather, Canada and Latin America have supplied some of the crude oil from which U.S. refineries have produced the vital fuels and the raw materials for making a wide variety of "synthetic" products. In fact, these oil-based synthetics have constituted the broad basis of new product development since the end of the Second World War; and aluminum and plastics have increasingly replaced steel and wood as raw material for an even larger list of consumer goods: furniture, important auto components, office equipment, appliance parts of all kinds, etc. Synthetics has driven cotton from its preeminent place in the production of clothing; replaced rubber as the key material for the production of vehicular tires and tubing for industrial as well as consumer use; and competed with wood as the primary raw material in furniture-making.

Thus, threatened shortages in oil-based chemicals have a wide impact on the entire economy. With the advent of plastics, the uses of the old materials have changed. Wood is now used chiefly for paper production and homes. Although the importance of cotton has declined relatively, it has now become the basis for more expensive clothing and household furnishings. It can be said, therefore, that U.S. research and development of petroleum has resulted in the replacement of many raw materials which were formerly imported.

I

The food crisis is even more surprising than the so-called energy crisis. The important historical function of cheap food has been to make possible relatively cheap wages. Even though U.S. wages have always been higher than in Europe and other industrial areas, these wages have been low in comparison with the productivity of American workers. Until recently, the proportion of machinery to labor has been highest in the U.S. among major industrial countries. The work culture in the United States has always been speeded up compared to all other countries, including Japan. Nowhere has the cult of efficiency sunk deeper roots than in the U.S. But Americans have always taken for granted our huge supplies of cheap food. We are accustomed to eating well as a nation. The beef consumption of American factory workers has historically been the envy of working classes of all capitalist countries, and the aspiration of developing nations.

The achievements of American agriculture, taken for granted for the past half-century, remain the unseen basis of much of American prosperity. Historically, the ability of the American economy to solve the agricultural "problem" has determined the pattern of industrial development. Low food and cotton prices drove millions off the farm. But they also created space for the mass consumption of durable goods that have become the bedrock of U.S. economic growth. For most years after the Second World War, blue-collar and white-collar workers spent less than half their income on food and clothing. For many, these necessities accounted for about 25 percent of the average wage or salary. This windfall meant that Americans spent the greater part of their income on homes, cars, appliances and other high-priced durable goods. The immense expansion of the "capital goods" industries in this country, especially steel, electrical manufacturing and machine tools, is directly attributable to the significance of the structure of average income. In turn, the capacity of the mass of workers to buy consumer durables has rested, until now, on the amazing productivity of American agriculture and the key extractive industries such as oil and coal.

Between 1946 and 1957 the amount of personal income spent on food and clothing increased by one-third.[1] Discounting the year 1946, when production of such goods as homes and automobiles was just resuming on a mass scale, in the ten years between 1947 and 1957 the consumption of automobiles rose nearly 300 percent and of homes about 270 percent. Actually, the proportion of personal consumption spent on food and clothing declined, while an increasing proportion of income went for autos, appliances and owner-occupied, nonfarm homes. In fact, the historical "crisis" of American agriculture has never been the problem of insufficient production as in the Soviet Union or Great Britain, but too much production relative to demand.

"Overproduction" of food and cotton was recognized as a national problem in the years just prior to the First World War. The price of cotton had remained stable for most of the nineteenth century. As America's major export crop until 1910, cotton was an important source for the formation of capitalism, and helped to generate America's phenomenal economic growth after the First World War. The export of food was an important source of economic growth as well. Durost and Barton have shown that "by 1900 exports of farm products were almost three times as large as in 1870, and the value of agricultural exports was 25% of the realized gross farm income."[2]

The enormous expansion of rail transportation and the increase in the nation's population and mechanization combined to help agricultural production expand by 143 percent between 1870 and 1900. In the next twenty years cropland area continued to increase, but at a much slower annual rate than the previous period. The First World War helped agricultural output to resume its vigorous pace of expansion, which continued into the 1920s. But in the middle of the decade farming hit bad times. The export rate slowed down considerably as prices of agricultural commodities fell on the world market. There was a relative world wide overproduction and new countries began to export agricultural products. Cotton was hardest hit even before the depression of the 1930s knocked the bottom out from under the whole agricultural market. American farmers, who had depended on the world market for an important part of their income, suddenly found themselves dependent on the domestic market in a greater measure than ever before. With the end of the high tide of immigration in the 1920s and the intensification of mechanized farming, many small producers found it impossible to remain in business.

As food and cotton prices fell, the first years of the depression witnessed a huge glut of these commodities on the market. This economic slump was accompanied by a steep rise of mortgage foreclosures. The aim of government policy during the 1930s was to limit the production of agricultural products in order to keep prices high and profits stable. The problem of agriculture was universally perceived as one of overproduction. Even though Roosevelt's Secretary of Agriculture, Henry Wallace, remarked ruefully that "to have to destroy a growing crop is a shocking commentary on our civilization," this was the heart of the New Deal farm policy. In August 1933, ten million acres of growing cotton were destroyed, six million baby pigs were slaughtered in September, and millions of bushels of wheat and other grains were dumped in order to keep prices up. But these dramatic measures were only the beginning.

What Broadus Mitchell [3] termed "planned scarcity" became the hallmark of government policy. Farmers were rewarded for retiring lands from cultivation, for growing crops that could not be brought to market for sale, and for combining to keep prices high through trade agreements between producers' cooperatives, processors and distributors. After the early days of "plowing up" grains and killing young animals, the Agricultural Adjustment Administration (the New Deal's main agency for controlling prices and production) established a structure that effectively cut production of nearly all commodities—with a little help from one of the most severe droughts in important farm regions in the 1934-1935 crop years. The intention of the AAA was to set up local organizations of farmers to administer themselves; however, most of the local committees established to plan the control mechanisms were dominated by large farmers. In the end, voluntary restrictions on output did not work. Despite material incentives to restrict production some crops were produced in larger quantities than desired by the government. A tax was levied against crops that were in excess of established quotas.

Many economists expected that the Depression of the 1930s would resume after the Second World War; the brief interlude of full employment created by the mobilization of all labor and material resources to produce war goods was not expected to carry over into the postwar years. In the eyes of many experts, the high production and profits generated by the war economy would inevitably give way to a slump.

Even though there were recessions in 1949-50, 1954 and

1958 that were serious enough, postwar America was not to experience the expected really deep slump. The severe downturn did not occur for three principal reasons: first, the most immediate source of economic buoyancy came from the savings of members of the armed forces and the work force, neither of which had been able to spend their money during the days of wartime shortages. Eleven million members of the armed forces returned from the war in dire need of housing, clothing and many other necessities.

Second, American credit helped make Europe an important market for U.S. capital investment as well as all types of goods. The destruction of significant sectors of Europe's industrial plant, the ravages brought about by the bombings and the scorched earth policy of the sinking Nazi war machine produced a severe contraction of arable land on the European continent. Of course, the United States government and corporations did not merely provide relief and long-term loans. In crucial industries, such as data processing, automobile manufacturing, iron and steel, and electronics, U.S. corporations became partners in European firms as the price of recovery assistance. Just as U.S. and German chemical corporations had entered partnership before World War II in such matters as control over patents, price agreements and joint stock ownership, the United States used its swollen capital resources after the War to penetrate more deeply into European industry.

The third reason why a depression failed to materialize immediately following this orgy of consumption of the postwar years is that instead of dismantling the U.S. war machine, American policy-makers discovered a new enemy: the Soviet Union. The ideology of anticommunism replaced antifascism as the raison d'être of permanent war preparations. Besides the need to equip the large American occupation forces in Europe and Asia, the United States government began to stockpile all types of military weapons several years prior to the Korean War of 1950, which made hot the cold war controversies of the previous three years. Permanent war industries became a major mechanism to forestall postwar depressions and to ensure steady levels of economic growth.

The federal government stepped in once more to shape the direction of the postwar recovery, just as it had shaped the direction of the slow recovery from the Depression. But now government policy was not aimed so much at restriction of output and maintenance of high prices through trade agreements. Instead, postwar federal aid to business created a climate favorable to investment and its concomitant economic growth. American foreign policy was aimed at rebuilding Europe and strengthening the role of the United States as a creditor nation. The intervention of American corporations in the economic and political life of Europe actually began with the First World War. The U.S. government extended credit to the Allies for the purchase of both war materiel and basic foodstuffs. After the war, the U.S. refused to honor its promise to forgive its allies for the war debt. Instead, it demanded payment in the form of concessions for U.S. business interests in European industry, or cash.

The process was repeated on an even wider scale after World War II. But the payback was not only cash, the European allies were also required to yield to their American benefactors a great measure of control over their own resources. America's intervention was cloaked in philanthropic programs that belied their intentions. The Marshall Plan, named for President Truman's Secretary of State and former chairman of the Joint Chiefs of Staff, was established ostensibly to help European economic recovery. The Truman doctrine of military containment of

Russia was the ideological rationale for maintaining a huge force of American troops in Europe after the cessation of shooting. Under the Truman Doctrine America also became the great organizer of the holy crusade against godless communism. Hundreds of thousands of U.S. troops, pockets bulging with dollars, stood guard at the borders between "East" and "West," while Europeans learned to drink Coca-Cola and dance to American pop music.

Big farmers welcomed ecumenical foreign policy as yet another forestalling operation. Butter, eggs and wheat found their way to government-owned storage bins. The federal government paid top dollars for these commodities but did not distribute food to starving peoples without strings. Better to keep the butter in storage as a tactical weapon against the invasion of the Reds into the sacred lands of Western civilization. When the Communist Party threatened to capture power in collaboration with its left-socialist allies in Italy, food became an important political force to retard the decline of the West. The wheat surpluses were used directly as an electoral weapon and successfully forestalled calamity. Indians achieved independence from Britain, but among the conditions of food aid from the United States was a pro-Western though non-aligned attitude toward the emerging East-West conflict.

Farm surpluses became an instrument of foreign policy and an object of intense political struggle at home. Despite the growing market for U.S. agricultural products, "farm interests" insisted that the price supports and subsidy programs of the Depression era be maintained, lest the demand signal another tragedy like the bad old days. Meanwhile, despite prosperity for the bigger farm, the migrations of smaller farmers to the city continued unabated. The old sharecropping system of the South—which had successfully contained millions of blacks in the tobacco and cotton fields after the Civil War abolished "slavery"—succumbed to the tractor and growing competition from other countries, principally the Middle East and India. Grain and cattle producers were affected by mechanization as well. The cost of operating a farm rose sharply after World War II and it became clear that even though farm prices did not plunge during the 1950s (and in fact rose somewhat during the late 1940s) food, cotton and tobacco remained fairly cheap compared to the prices of everything else.

Low prices for agricultural commodities meant that the land had to yield increased crops in order to make a profit. The cash payments farm owners received from the federal government were invested in new machines. But the latest technologies of farm production were only economical on large tracts of cultivated land. Thus, concentration of grain and cattle production in fewer hands became almost inevitable in the postwar period. The rate of profit on agriculture, traditionally less than industrial profits, could sustain farmers only where the volume of production was sufficient to offset low income on each acre of land. The small farmers could not afford the new machines that were developed by agricultural implement corporations with an eye to large holdings. In many cases, the purchase of such equipment made no sense for small farms anyway. Those farmers who did not become agricultural laborers after the War went to work in the city. For some time, many of them held onto their small farms as a supplement to their factory wages. But gradually, the struggle proved too much for the overwhelming majority of small farmers. By 1960 the "family" farmer, i.e. self-employed working farmers, had all but disappeared.

As farm output rose, the number of commercial farms decreased more than 2 percent each year from 1939 to 1960. By 1970 the number of commercial farms had decreased to 1.5 million from 3 million farms thirty years earlier. Yet productivity on the land had increased faster than productivity increases for the economy as a whole. Agricultural productivity rose about 5 percent a year during most of the postwar period compared to a 3.4 percent increase of productivity for the economy as a whole during the period from 1940 to 1970.[4] The farm laborer replaced the working farm owner as the characteristic producer in American agriculture.

Yet the myth of the "farm" interest persisted, despite the fact that most commercial farms were no longer owned by family-producers. The farm interest became almost identical with the general corporate interest since control over agriculture had passed to the banks, large conglomerates such as Tenneco and ITT, and huge, vertically integrated food corporations which had extended their influence to all branches of the industry including growing, processing, distribution and marketing.

Agricultural consolidation had a profound effect on other aspects of industrial development. Small farms were abandoned, and the large growers were able to mechanize almost all farming and sell millions of acres for other uses. Land became available for real estate development, particularly for residential and industrial construction. The organizational transformation of farming provided much of the impetus for the dispersal of American industry and, with it, new patterns of living. The concentration of America's population in the center cities brought about by the industrial revolution of the late nineteenth century was being reversed.

In the postwar period, changing patterns of social and economic life were guaranteeing a long-term future for the automobile and all the commodities it used. America did not only enter the world market as the most important colonial nation, it also exploited its own internal market on an unprecedented scale. From 1870 to the end of World War II, industrialization had been accompanied by urban concentration of the population. The greater part of U.S. industry was concentrated in a score of industrial areas, whose core was the large city. Great cities grew from the centralization of industrial wealth. Chicago, Detroit, Pittsburgh and others were identified with the expansion of specific industries. There were industrial suburbs, but most often these were mere extensions of the parameters of the city itself.

After the War, it became evident that America's planners were facing momentous choices. The cities required renewal if they were to remain the industrial heartland of the nation. The demand for housing had reached explosive proportions since the old stock of slum and tenement housing had deteriorated rapidly during the Depression. Besides, war veterans were unwilling to return to these old neighborhoods unless living conditions had improved. The promises of the wartime patriotic appeals had to be fulfilled lest the classical radicalization of the citizen military upset existing power relationships. Among the most striking features of the War was that it was fought by a higher proportion of the working class than ever before; they were conscripted on the basis of a pledge by the ruling groups to make life better following the victory over fascism and this pledge caused worry among those who were not sure how to make good on it.

The pattern of the dispersal of the textile industry provided one model for corporate decision-makers. In the 1920s the cotton textile industry, which had been heavily concentrated in New England, solved its expansion problems by removing itself almost entirely to the South. New England factory towns were left desolate and abandoned in the wake of this textile relocation. The industry was essentially gone from the rivers of the northern New England region by 1949, and these areas have never fully recovered from the loss. The cities of New Bedford, Fall River and Lawrence in Massachusetts, Biddeford and Saco in Maine, and Manchester, New Hampshire, are still marked by half-filled or empty red brick factory buildings that stand as grim reminders of the past.

The case of autos and steel was more complicated. In the first place, the capital investment required to construct a steel mill was much larger than that required by textile, shoe or garment manufacture, which had followed the textile industry to the tax-free, land-free, water-free southern precincts. Unlike the weak textile and shoe unions, the unions in these basic industries had, by the late 1930s, become too powerful to allow the industry to move swiftly without substantial protest. Instead of closing down Pittsburgh and Gary, the steel industry giants chose a more moderate path. Their new plants would not be located in the central urban areas, but would be placed in outlying areas and the older cities would be allowed to deteriorate slowly. The auto industry followed the same policy as did rubber, electrical and the older sectors of the chemical industry. By 1960, Detroit, which once housed 90 percent of all auto manufacturing, had shrunk to 50 percent of auto production.

In the 1950s some old plants were closed, but nearly all new plants were built outside the central cities. The rapidly expanding chemical industry, which made the synthetic fibers that were replacing natural fibers for clothing and household furnishings, and plastics that replaced heavier and costlier metals, also chose to build away from the cities.

The plans of industry direct the plans of government. Instead of rejuvenating the cities by developing new housing for workers and for poor people, and creating mass transit systems to make travel within the city easier, government planners began to accommodate the decisions of corporations in terms of industrial location. Instead of mass transit, the most important "social" measure of the federal government after World War II was the highway program that reconstructed America's roadways to allow millions of cars to carry workers to and from their jobs, now located in the middle of former corn or wheat fields or an old chicken farm.

Given the new structure of industrial location, the fate of the housing emphasis was sealed. The brave plans of the New Deal—never realized beyond a few token programs—to reconstruct the ghettos and slums and produce decent housing at low cost for millions of families were quietly shelved. The token federal housing program was kept as a concession to the vast numbers of persons left behind and to the liberals who still believed in the myths of the social system. Right after the War, the Truman administration showed in which direction it was going on the vital issue of housing. In the guise of making good its promises, the Administration enacted a loan program to permit veterans to buy single family private housing at low interest rates. The Congress moved swiftly at the Administration's initiative and the private building industry, which had suffered sorely during the Depression, was instantly revived. Of course, the same banks that made the individual loans to potential homeowners, were making loans to building contractors as well. The federal government insured these loans as well as the mortgages and a new industrial sector was born.

## II

The veterans loan program, cloaked in the garb of social welfare legislation, was actually one of the most important decisions determining the shape of the entire economy in the postwar period. It was a key tool in the transition from wartime to peacetime production because it provided capital for housing construction. But even more importantly, it had a profound effect on the way people were to live, the way in which energy resources would be consumed, and the configuration of consumer goods production and consumption. The production of durable goods, particularly automobiles and appliances was given an enormous shot in the arm.

The infrastructure was established for new patterns of production, new modes of living and a new culture. Within a decade after the War, the rush to the suburbs and its peripheries had escalated to a gallop. White working class people and a sprinkling of blacks were offered jobs and homes in the suburbs. They required automobiles to get everywhere. The combination of industrial and government planning together with financial institutions determined the configuration of American life for decades to come. As long as oil flowed freely from domestic as well as Latin American wells, as long as this fuel could be refined by modern technologies, as long as capital guaranteed the dominance of the automobile as the major means of travel, industry would not be imprisoned within the arcane vertical structures made necessary by land shortages in large cities. Traditionally the city had been built along the water. Water power and transportation made this necessary. The old need to stay near the water was overcome by overland travel as well as the advent of electric power made possible by the vast quantities of coal, which could be produced from the apparently limitless reserves found throughout the country.

Under the pressure of technological modernization and the lure of the hinterlands that offered many cash incentives to relocate, many sectors of American industry headed for the woods in the 1950s and 1960s. The government provided the infrastructural necessities: modern highways, guaranteed mortgages for ticky-tacky one-family homes, and, of course, a high level of government spending for military purposes that became a vital component of the sales of almost all major corporations.

In the midst of the transformation of the face of the nation, especially the obliteration of farmlands, the country was suffused with nostalgia for the good old days of small town and country living. The great musical comedies of the 1940s and 1950s, *Oklahoma, Carousel, Brigadoon, The Most Happy Fella, Annie Get Your Gun* and many others, evoked the romantic memory of a bygone era, of cowboys and farmers and quaint countryside. The American musical stage, which also influenced the character of the huge, expensive movie productions of the era, became the repository of the images of an America that had rapidly been destroyed. Of course, the musical performed other relevant contemporary functions. Conjuring up the Old West was a fruitful way to recapture patriotism in a period when various. war scars were a permanent part of the landscape. Moreover, the compulsion to "escape" had not receded from mass audiences despite the "good times" of postwar prosperity. The quality of everyday life kept lessening. Only the romance of agriculture could revive the sense of richness that had been lost amid the chaotic senselessness of the suburban sprawl.

Since the 1920s when the mass consumption of cars became a central feature of economic and social life, Americans have been a peripatetic people. But these tendencies, accelerated by the frantic search for work and security during the Depression, hit a peak in the postwar era. With the construction of the superhighway (from technologies learned by wartime road building), shopping centers sprouted and we stopped walking, except on the job because distances had become too great.

The car changed the face of our commercial as well as industrial life. We began to eat food in our cars, in quaint restaurants called drive-ins where, as portrayed in the film *American Graffiti*, waitresses called "car-hops" used roller-skates to serve hamburgers, french fries and milk-shakes. Instead of hanging out in drugstores, teenagers met in the parking spaces of these instant water holes. The old ice-cream parlor, scene of many childhood pleasures of a bygone generation, became extinct toward the end of the 1950s only to be revived in the new bohemias of the center cities during the next decade as expensive tourist attractions—perhaps the first sign of the new nostalgia. Every major road housed a drive-in movie theater, often perched in a worked-out cornfield. There, young people explored the mysteries of the organism in dialectic combat with each other in the hospitable decor of the auto's interior and with the insects who were attracted by the smell of refreshments consisting of car-hop cuisine and human flesh. The term "strip" acquired a new significance in the American language when it was used to describe the miles of department stores and other commodity fairs on the highways. American highways have been built from the corpse of vast tracts of abandoned agricultural lands.

There is no need to rhapsodize the images of tall corn-stalks or willowy wheat plants to make vivid the loss represented by this transformation. The rise of the automobile, the one-family worker's house, the low-slung horizontal factory structure and the strip have become too much a routine feature of our field of vision to recall the way it used to be. The "country" was the summer refuge of my childhood. It was the respite from the ravages of brick and mortar that seemed inexorable except for the chance to escape to the trees and fields. As a child of the Depression, I was not aware that even the "summer camps" and the resorts were often mute signs that the countryside was declining. This decline was particularly evident in eastern New York and New England, regions that were never rich enough for bountiful commercial agriculture. I know now that even the Puritans and the Dutch had hard times trying to eke a living from the recalcitrant rock-based soil.

The resorts are still there, but they are fashioned from concrete as are most of the stores, gas stations and eating places. The city has spread to the countryside, narrowing the visual as well as social distinctions between the two. In some areas of the nation, the sprawl is even more lamentable because real estate developers have erected their housing developments and shopping plazas on hallowed ground. In the Middle West, in the bread basket of our nation, there is the same commercial blight, roads full of carbon monoxide, and sore, chaotic residential enclaves litter the horizon.

Food shortage? Consider the pattern of land use. Energy waste? How could it be otherwise when the crucial link of social and economic life is the automobile propelled by the internal-combustion engine, which burns more than six million barrels of gasoline every day, or two billion barrels a year. How can a society justify the use of one of our precious resources—space—for single-family homes that consume enormous quantities of electricity to power individually owned washing machines, dishwashers, blenders, not to mention the lighting of the home itself? The atomization of everyday existence is good for the production of coal, the vital fuel of electric power. Also for the heating-oil industry.

The family as a *consuming* unit has become more important than any of its traditional functions. The old roles performed by the ancestral farm have all but disappeared. No longer is the family at the center of the production of material necessities. Nor is the role of the family secure as the producer of social ideologies and values that prepare the child for wage labor, as the schools and mass culture move in to play a dominant role in the "socialization process." The family has become less and less an institution that is charged with the main responsibility for the education of the young. Instead, the social importance of the family is diminished to the physical caring and feeding of the child, and the transmission of the culture of consumption. The smaller the family, the more efficient it is in terms of the consumption of commodities. The nuclear family, which is both socially and physically isolated, is a perfect instrument for absorbing the junk of waste production. The less collective social life has become, the more functional small living units are in terms of the surplus generated by the mammoth economy.

Yet it cannot be said that the "surfeit of honey," an apt characterization by Russell Lynes, made life in the postwar era more satisfying. Writers lamented the emptiness of suburban life for the man in the gray-flannel suit. Vance Packard asked whether the measure of personal worth by the number and opulence of possession of consumer goods represented a trivialization of the culture. While workers sometimes reveled in their new homes and shiny appliances (both owned jointly with the banks), it did not take long for the middle class to experience a sense of loss for the very same reasons. Status could not be on the basis of occupation alone; it was necessary to own a bigger home and a more powerful car than your neighbor. Prestige was not to be found in creative labor nor even a job well done. Instead, distinction was measured by the size of backyards and swimming pools. Thorstein Veblen's observation that American society has become one of conspicuous consumption, may have been prophetic rather than descriptive in the years following World War I. But by the

1950s Veblen's notion of an invidious culture served as an adequate description of the present. The 1950s was the age of junk. It was a time when we collectively rediscovered the word "alienation." All objects seemed strangely foreign to us, most of all ourselves and our "loved ones." The American middle class could not rest content with its exterior pleasures; instead, it turned inward after a decade of uninterrupted accumulation. In the last years of the decade, the middle class began, more and more, to adopt the "jargon of authenticity." [5] It was searching for its own soul that seemed to have lost itself in the cacophony of consumerism.

The search for the authentic self forced the relatively affluent middle class into veritable orgies of self-examination. It was not only the therapy explosion that signified this phenomenon. The therapeutic experience extended to a new definition of personal relations as well. The ordinary world of commerce demanded that transactional relations be observed with the strictness of law. In "business" the middle class learned not to trust those with whom trading was done, and therefore public life could not provide the model for personal relations. The business world had to be accepted as part of nature. The individual had no control in this sphere and the rules of trade had eternal inevitability. The individual could exercise a measure of control in "private" life, e.g., the time away from work. Here, honesty could prevail. The "real" self could flourish in a way made impossible by the vicissitudes of daily labor where lies were represented as truths, where principle inevitably had to be sacrificed to expediency, where morality gave way to cash nexus.

Fritz Perls was among the prophets of the new authentic middle class. [6] His critique of the banality of the consumer society was focused on the ways in which persons became separated from themselves by the drive for social and bureaucratic success. Perls was neither a social critic nor a political leader. He was representative of a new genre among American intellectuals: the psychoanalyst for whom critical thought is preeminently useful as a prescription for personal conduct. Perls advised his patients and his reading public to adopt new ways of living in order to overcome the sense of isolation and despair shared by many Americans. He was a strong opponent of all kinds of compulsive behavior, especially the tendency among his natural constituents to seek public success without paying sufficient attention to their own needs. But he never demanded changes in the social structure as a precondition or concomitant to personal salvation. Among other things, Perls believed that eating was an important symptom of character: a person who chewed his food thoroughly possessed an important outlet for his aggressions and was less likely to act out against other persons. Similarly, training of our sense of taste may help develop our ability to make the elements of a rich life out of small daily activities.

But Perls was frustrated by the fact that the food offered in restaurants and other public eating places provided few opportunities to work out the basic psychological needs that he identified. One can hardly cultivate the sense of taste when most restaurant coffee resembles water more than anything else. The public marketplace offered few opportunities for healthy, aggressive mastication. People gulped their plastic food hurrying to and from work. There was no time for the preparation either of the digestive system or of appetizing dishes in a world where consumption itself became the object of human activity, and quantity rather than quality was the benchmark.

Perls found the private life to be no less alienating than public life. It became necessary for Perls and others seeking a fulfilling environment to create it themselves, rather than relying on the elements of existing social relationships. The formation of Esalen Institute signaled a new wave of encounter groups, therapy groups and other forms of non-individual ways to overcome the tenuousness of everyday existence without challenging its social roots. But those measures only increased the fragmentation of everyday life since they did not transform its basic structure. The middle class continued to lead their alienated success-oriented lives six days a week, but reserved a single day, a few weeks or a month for an authenticating marathon.

Accompanying the proliferation of new institutions devoted to helping individuals find their humanity through confrontation with others was a slowly rising recognition that chemically treated, processed food was merely the corporeal form of our mutual malaise. The new health-food industry promised to return food to its "natural" state rather than use artificial means to preserve it. Many even rebelled against chemically modified water and another industry came into being—bottled spring water. By the middle 1960s it was possible to construct an entire diet of bread, cheese, meat, eggs that escaped the older chemical processors in favor of a new commercial "health food" network.

Choked by our own prosperity, Americans began to experience a real fear of extinction. It appeared as if the evil forces of the commodity world were closing in on us. As the number of traffic accidents rose, and the quantity of carbon monoxide that filled the air increased, many voices were raised against unabated auto production and air travel. Responding to the middle class, the government required manufacturers to provide seat belts and emission controls as standard equipment on new automobiles and to limit the sulfur content of fuels—a heavy blow to the already hard-hit coal industry.

Meanwhile, auto production reached its historical pinnacle in 1965 when nearly 10 million cars were turned out in a single year, a figure around which production was to be maintained until 1973, 100 million cars glutting the streets and highways. More than 1.5 million owner-occupied new homes were being produced each year, necessitating the consumption of additional millions of barrels of oil and huge quantities of natural gas.

The traditional mode of personal travel, the railroad, deteriorated substantially in the two decades between 1950 and 1970. Henceforth transcontinental travelers would be required to change trains in Chicago. Gradually, more and more rail lines were retired, the railroad companies said, because only freight handling was still profitable by rail. Passenger transportation was a losing proposition. And, with the exception of commuter trains to and from the suburbs for work purposes, rusted rails lined the landscapes. Even the commuter trains were ill-kept, slow and often dangerous. The litany of complaints from irate train travelers became a commonplace feature of Letters to the Editor columns while ambitious suburban politicians promised instant relief if elected.

Meanwhile, the freeways and expressways became the world's largest parking lots especially during rush hours as large numbers of persons refused to risk the irritation and even their lives on unreliable commuter trains. There seemed to be a direct correlation between the rise of the automobile and the decline of the railroad. Rail corporations were given leave by federal agencies to improve their profit picture by discontinuing unprofitable passenger lines because the heart of government transportation policy was built around the requirements of the automobile and oil companies on the one hand, and the new industrial and residential patterns on the other. It is no accident that the only other important measure speeded through Congress to improve transportation was the federal airport construction program that provided sufficient funds to rebuild and expand almost every major airport in the country between 1955 and 1970.

Along with the antiwar protest and the civil rights struggle, the 1960s was also a decade when many Americans began to experience an exquisite sense of danger regarding the physical environment; nature appeared in full-throated revolt against man. The disturbances of the traditional balances between humans and their environment were believed to constitute a direct threat to life. The thrust of the so-called "ecology movement" won some victories in the halls of State and national legislatures and executive mansions. Evidence of oil spills polluting the coastlines of the country brought powerful demands for regulation of oil shipments. For a time, the powerful oil lobbies in Congress seemed to have reached their all-time ebb. Proposals for oil-drilling rights in offshore areas, pipeline construction across Alaska, and the use of public lands for a variety of industrial development projects by private industry languished hopelessly in congressional committees that had suddenly become frightened of the wrath of the environmentalists. For the first time in contemporary history, many were asking whether the sacred cow of economic growth should be eaten.

The 1973 energy crisis seemed to put America back on the high road of production exploitation. Government and corporate leaders abandoned plans for environmental protection. This was no time for utopian sentiment. Again it became the grave business of the country to achieve more goods needed by the economy. In the winter, announcements of mass layoffs in the automobile and chemical industries reinforced this attitude. As unemployment rose, "put America back to work" replaced "clean up the air" as the rallying cry of the nation. As if asleep,

Congress approved the Alaska pipeline as federal agencies raised permissible levels of pollution in fuels. With the growing shortages of fuel, motorists were willing to pay higher prices for gasoline, and home owners for heating oil. Oil tankers carrying crude oil were diverted in December to military installations and markets offering higher prices for the now scarce brown gold. At the same time, Senate hawks were protesting that oil shipments were being diverted from military installations to foreign ports.

III

The American philosophy has become one of novelty. Karl Marx said that the tendency of capital is to revolutionize constantly the means of production. American capital has added to this constant revolutionizing the proliferation of the number and variety of consumer goods. What we have learned about the concept of "need" from the past twenty-five years is that these human needs in themselves are socially determined. That sexual and social needs are manipulated by advertisements piped in through the television tube, the billboard and the car radio, requires no further elaboration here. What must be discussed, however, is the way in which needs are produced by the structure of everyday existence. The structure is not a product of nature or human evolution. Instead, the specific configuration of the family, isolated in a small dwelling, located in a non-place and connected only by electronic and mechanical means to the social world, is now a product of both intentional and unintentional collaboration between business and government. We can observe with the advantages of hindsight the decision-making process that led to the objective possibility of an energy and food crisis. The profit criterion as a means to allocate both human and natural resources becomes enormously efficient in the short run and a major disaster over the long haul.

But merely sketching the objective circumstances that explain the enormous wastefulness of the way in which we produce and consume goods is not the same as giving credence to the claim that real shortages exist in relation to current social arrangements. For it may be possible that the same constellation of interests that is capable of transforming the entire shape of our past lives by legislation, executive edict, and administrative choice may also be able to manipulate the present and future to correspond to their imperatives.

There is no powerful consumer movement in the United States, and any other organized forces capable of sustaining political action to deal with the crises were either part of the problem (as in the instance of the giant corporations) or completely immobilized, as was the trade union movement. The configuration of economic development that created new, isolated ways of living had become a powerful means to force mass acceptance of the new situation. Privatization disarmed the victims. By the end of 1973 some unions, particularly the independent United Electrical Workers, were making valiant efforts to mobilize their members and other unionists to protest the higher utility rates that were ostensibly caused by higher fuel prices. The impulse to protest was present, but the means seemed to be lacking for effective struggle. As far as the rest of the trade union movement was concerned, action was confined to the bargaining table or to feeble efforts to convince Congress to move. The perfidy of almost the entire labor movement was indicated by its refusal to call political strikes, demonstrations, or even mass lobbying activities against the price squeeze.

Given the absence of an articulate opposition, the

concept of individual choice in the economic sphere became anachronistic. None of the decisions that shaped the postwar era—from the Federal Housing Act, the Highway program, and the plan for industrial dispersal, to the concentration of American agriculture into fewer and fewer hands—was inevitable. The helplessness of the American people is itself a by-product of the invisible process of corporate and government policies, including the successful ideological and administrative integration of the trade unions into the corporate order.

# 2

# Butter from Boeing, Ham from ITT

The most striking aspect of the many price increases of the past several years has been the especially sharp rise in the price of food. True, food prices have been inching upward steadily since the end of the Second World War. From 1967 to 1972 the average annual increase was about 4 percent, which was somewhat higher than the general postwar yearly price hikes.[1] But the 20.6 percent jump in the fifteen months between June 1972 and September 1973 represented the biggest boost since 1951.

Most consumers found themselves in a severe crunch. Hemmed in by high house or rent payments and car payments on one hand, and heavy federal, state and local taxes on the other, working people found themselves faced with a major choice: either take a second job (if available) or eat less and cheaper. The trouble with the former option was that jobs were becoming scarce in 1973. Unemployment rates were rising and the rate of economic growth slowing down. By early 1974, the growth rate was approaching zero and government economists were predicting a light decline in production for the first half of the year. In short, many workers were hanging on to their first job, hoping that the layoffs due to the so-called "energy crisis" would not affect them. As for the strategy of eating cheaper, it turned out that not only had meat and poultry prices climbed steeply, but the price of bread and other staples had risen almost as much. There was no way out. Even substituting carbohydrates for protein did not help. As a consequence, the public had less money to spend for durable goods such as cars, washing machines and TV sets.

Of all the "crises," the food crisis had an aspect of terror. After all, even for many persons in lower income brackets the plenitude of food and its relative variety constituted an important source of psychological security. As if to underscore the disintegration of the assumptions of daily life, food was not only expensive but some types of food were actually becoming scarce. Hoarding meat became a commonplace. People began to shop in bulk rather than run to the nearest grocery store for a quart of milk and a loaf of bread. Shopping now became a serious life activity for many who simply never considered the problem of getting nourishment as something to be planned.

The old car could only stand a limited number of patchings. The house needed a new roof. Instead of abandoning it to the next generation of property-poor people, homeowners were inclined to repair the old homestead. But it meant that a second (or third) mortgage would have to be loaned from the bank. In 1973 people found that even home mortgages were scarce. Savings had declined a bit but, more important, commercial banks and savings and loan companies that had traditionally provided the main sources of mortgage money were no longer investing in housing to the same degree as before. Instead, they were putting depositors' money into more profitable businesses such as agriculture, which *Business Week* concluded was America's "greatest growth industry" of 1972.[2] Since capital flows to the most profitable sources of investment and ordinarily is not sentimental, the huge profits on investments in agriculture contributed to the lack of loan capital for housing.

These huge profits in agriculture that began to be earned in late 1972 and 1973 are the other side of the coin of high food prices. The real issues are: Why did agriculture, long a relatively low profit industry, suddenly become lucrative to investors? Why are prices spurting? The most paradoxical question of all: How can agriculture be the leading "growth industry" while there seems to be a shortage of food?

I

There are two obvious explanations for the sudden gallop in the prices of meat and grains, the staples of many American diets. The first is a conventional argument for high prices: bad crop years create shortages that drive up the prices of foodstuffs, and there were some bad crop years in the early 1970s. Droughts and floods in some sections of the country and an unusually high proportion of crop failures due to pests limited the flow of goods to the wholesalers. According to this line of reasoning, given adequate weather conditions the high prices of food created by temporary shortages will induce farmers to plant more acres and return the supply to its normal levels in the next year. Which will in turn lead to lower prices over the long run.

However, this view overlooks that the cultivation of

land depends on more than the law of supply and demand. Since 1933, the amount of land under cultivation has been regulated by government incentives to persuade farmers not to grow food, but rather to retire food producing lands. After direct government subsidies to farmers agreeing to plow under crops and to leave the soil uncultivated were ruled unconstitutional in 1935, Congress passed a law allowing the same practices to go on under the rubric of "soil conservation." County agents of the United States Department of Agriculture were authorized to pay farmers to retire croplands and restrict livestock production where the danger of soil erosion was determined. The purpose of federal incentives was clearly to prevent food and other agricultural products from becoming so plentiful on the market as to force prices downward. In essence, the "law of supply and demand" could not be relied upon ever again.

Furthermore, since the degree of mechanization of American agriculture exceeds that of any other country, the productivity of farm labor has made "supply" chronically larger than "demand." Increased productivity is graphically illustrated by the following: In 1910, it was estimated that 147 labor hours were required to produce a bushel of wheat.[3] By 1960 4 hours of labor turned out the same amount. In fifty years, labor productivity on the farm had increased nearly 40 times. While the average annual productivity rate increased 3 percent for American industry as a whole, agriculture productivity was rising 5 to 6 percent a year. Even though the number of farms has steadily declined since 1935 when there were almost seven million of them, the problem of crop surpluses has beleaguered both the agriculture sector and government policy since the late 1890s, remaining a serious concern of national policy during the New Deal and after the War.

As incredible as it sounds, "surplus" is the key word in the history of American agriculture. Yet it has become synonymous with the concept of "crisis." As William Appleman Williams has argued, the tendency for farm surpluses to exceed consumption has been a crucial impulse toward United States expansion in the twentieth century.[4] Even if the search for markets has often been undertaken in the name of capital, rather than commodity export and the need to find raw materials to supply the rising manufacturing industries in the United States, farm interests—so Williams shows—figured powerfully in the shaping of United States policies of expansion.

In the 1890s 25 percent of all agricultural production went for export and this tendency to produce for the world market has been central to the fortunes of the American farm sector ever since the 1930s. The export of farm goods was facilitated by government subsidies when New Deal diplomacy attempted to accelerate the disposal of farm surpluses through foreign trade agreements which provided for the import of manufactured goods and such cash crops as coffee. The heart of government agricultural policies has not only been price supports for domestic . production, but also the two-price system. Exports have been assisted by government programs aimed at subsidizing the favorable competitive position of American-grown goods. Government purchases of agricultural products were meant to restrict the quantity of food on the market and keep prices relatively high.

So much for the natural disasters argument. Not since 1934, when a widespread drought actually aided the basic New Deal objective of restricted farm production, has nature cooperated.

The second explanation for skyrocketing prices asserts that the recent Soviet wheat deal was responsible for the suddenness of the price hikes. The facts about the deal are fairly straightforward. In a 1972 bumper crop year, the United States negotiated the sale of 440 million bushels of wheat and 267 million bushels of other grains to the Soviet Union at bargain prices. According to the Department of Agriculture, the deal was made in order to dispose of huge farm surpluses. It was also important as a major means of overcoming the more than six-billion-dollar balance of payments deficit incurred in 1972.

The wheat sale absorbed 25 percent of the 1972 United States production. Exports of corn and soybeans, used not only for human consumption but for livestock feed as well, also reached epic proportions. Of the 5.8 billion bushels of corn produced in the same year, 1.2 billion were earmarked for export, including to the Soviet Union. Soybean exports rose to more than 52 percent of the total production by 1973, up 4 percent from 1972, which was a big year for shipments, especially to Europe and Japan.

By 1973 U.S. exporters held contracts totaling more than half the annual production of wheat. Of course, not all contracts were destined to be filled in a single year or out of current stocks. But the rise in the world demand for grains quickly solved the so-called "surplus" problem here in the United States. By employing its two-price system, whereby prices for exports are lower than the price in the domestic market, the United States government had made food a critical factor in overcoming sagging trade balances.

But rising food prices were not confined to such items as bread and spaghetti. Rising exports of grains, that would otherwise have been used for livestock feed, forced cattle growers to pay more at home for feed, forcing prices of beef, pork and chicken to new levels. In the year ending September, 1972, beef prices increased by 28 percent, pork rose by more than 50 percent and poultry jumped by more than 65 percent.

The international clamor for United States grains helped force domestic prices up, despite government export supports, which amounted to $150 million in 1973. Storage bins were emptied; European countries and Japan especially competed for U.S. grain. As the world market price rose, other countries began to use grains as a major means of accumulating hard-to-get capital. For example, Brazil tore up coffee plantations and began to grow soybeans, almost all for export. In spring 1973, a *Newsweek* correspondent reported from Naples: "Italians have found the wheat supply solution [of rationing wheat] threatening civil peace . . . Neapolitans rioted in the streets for several days last month when bakers closed up because the government's price controls wouldn't permit them to pass on higher wheat costs . . ." Japan sent envoys to the Middle East to garner exclusive oil deals, but also cornered the market on Middle Eastern wool.

President Nixon finally acted. Soybean exports were controlled, much to the chagrin of European food growers who expected a windfall of relatively cheap livestock feed to help stem inflationary pressures by lowering production costs. After all, the United States produces 73 percent of the world's soybeans and it will take years before this high protein food can be economically grown by European countries or supplied by Latin American countries now producing sugar or coffee but willing to convert to grains.

Meanwhile, French government members were becoming increasingly angry at the growing competition for U.S. grains. The French Premier accused the United States of using food as a diplomatic weapon against its European rivals. Higher food costs were creating internal tensions within Common Market countries as workers demanded wage increases to offset the rampant inflation which, in turn, was producing stagnation within West German, French and British economies.

The Soviet wheat deal, surely a catalyst for pushing up

food prices, cannot be held strictly accountable for the increases. It was the world monetary crisis in general, and the United States balance of trade problems in particular, that played an important part in the food shortages that began to appear at home during late fall 1972.

Millions of words have been written about such matters as "dollar devaluation," "balance of payments," and "gold crisis." Ordinary people are often confused by these terms because they are used by businessmen, journalists, economists and government officials in a bewildering manner. Actually, the international problems of U.S. capitalism, although complex, are far from incomprehensible.

Our story of the food "crisis" leads directly to the general crisis of United States international relations, because the immense size of American agricultural production, although limited by government programs that have encouraged crop reductions, are still large enough to provide a significant portion of United States overseas trade as well as meet the consumption levels of 210 million Americans.

Since the end of World War I, when the United States emerged as the most powerful "creditor" nation in the world, the dollar has been the informal currency of international exchange. Even during the Depression when the United States domestic production declined precipitously, the exports of goods and capital was the hallmark of American foreign policy. Through the reciprocal trade agreements of the 1930s and 1940s, America used its farm surpluses to balance the growing volume of imports from other countries.[5]

The importance of the so-called balance of trade cannot be underestimated for the stability of currency. As the volume of trade rises and becomes a more important component of total production within a country, inflation becomes more and more dependent on whether the total value of goods and capital exported exceeds the amount imported. Capital invested in other countries as well as commodities purchased from overseas sources means that quantities of dollars are being accumulated in foreign banks and other exchange institutions. Common mythology to the contrary, the price of gold still regulates currency values and influences the fortunes of international commerce. If the economy of the United States, for instance, is relatively secure, demands are not made to exchange dollars for gold. But if the balances are excessively weighted against the United States, then other countries, and their merchants and bankers in particular, begin to demand gold in exchange for dollars. In turn, the price of gold rises and the dollar decreases in value.

Three important developments in the 1960s transformed the once secure position of the United States in the world economy. First, the size of United States capital investments overseas increased as profit margins within the United States failed to match opportunities in the countries of Europe as well as Asia and Latin America. Part of the reason for increased investments was the lower wages offered overseas. Equally important, however, was the relatively unrestricted use of natural resources allowed by countries such as Spain and Italy as well as Latin American nations—natural resources that could be exploited at little or no cost beyond those of exploration and operations. The tax structure of developing nations is far more favorable to business than even the windfall concessions made to many corporations in the United States. Supplies of water, electricity and other services needed for transportation and production are made available at exceedingly low prices. When the political conditions of Latin America, the Middle East, and Western Europe stabilized after the turbulence of the late 1950s and early 1960s, the "climate" for investment improved. In the later years of the decade, the international "runaway" shop was not just a distant specter for American workers; it had become a reality. Not only did U.S.-based corporations choose to expand overseas rather than within the United States; many chose not to replace old plants within the United States and instead built elsewhere. All this meant that the United States industrial base became relatively narrower and dollars piled up overseas.

The Vietnam war, too, which reached its zenith from 1964 to 1969, was a direct cause of the growing weakness of the dollar. The combination of 500,000 U.S. troops in Asia and millions of tons of equipment and vast quantities of U.S. military aid to the various regimes of South Vietnam—all served to accelerate the pace of dollar exports. The export of capital was not the only objective of the war; the war was fought, in part, to protect nearly six billion dollars of American oil and other industrial investments and future prospects for natural-resource development in Southeast Asia.

And finally, Europe, which had absorbed an enormous share of U.S. capital and agricultural surpluses after the war, began to require fewer American goods as its own economies became more self-sustaining. The formation of the European Common Market at the end of the 1950s quickened the pace of its relative self-sufficiency. United States capital was still flowing to European industry, but exports of American goods, especially food and heavy equipment, declined sharply after the mid 1950s. Even though the influence of U.S. corporations remained unabated and in fact became greater as American financial and industrial giants went into "partnership" with weaker European firms, monetary and trade competition between nations remained.

The paradox of closer economic integration of Europe with the United States and the increasing conflict between Europe and this country is a distinguishing feature of our era. On the one hand, corporate ownership has burst traditional boundaries. The complex of multinational corporations, characteristically based within the United States, now consistute a supra state. The sovereignty of nations has not only been undermined by the increasing number of international and internationally controlled corporations: While these corporations make their own laws and influence governments to adapt public law to their particular private needs, they are also capable of mobilizing armies to fight their wars, manipulating currencies to fit their requirements and synchronizing their own activities independent of most legal restraints.

On the other hand, the world polity is still organized on the principle of nation states. Each nation still issues its own currency and there remain large sectors of their economies that operate within their respective internal markets and have little direct relations with the overseas activities of the multinationals. Even though the multinational corporations within the United States have exercised decisive influence over the course of U.S. foreign policy, in order to shape it to meet their particular needs, other business groups less connected to the international economy act to oppose the hegemony of the multinationals. The contestants are unevenly matched, since the multinationals are among the richest and most powerful of the corporations. Yet their actions affect the destiny of nations as well as their own affairs.

And it is this conflict between multinationals and national business groups such as retailers and some manufacturers that has, in the broad sense, affected issues such as devaluation of the dollar, the gold crisis and other international monetary issues. The dual structure of supranational corporations* and nation states at first appears anomalous. The competition between the multinationals and the national corporations within a given country is severe but not at all equal.The international corporations have tightened their grip over their respective governments since the beginning of the 1960s and have wielded national governmental power to serve their particular interests almost at will. This development is especially pronounced in the United States, the seat of many multinational corporations. Especially powerful in this respect have been the oil, chemical and automobile companies.

Yet nation states represent more than a curious lag between the actual emergence of the internationalization of capital and the persistence of apparently arcane national political structures with roots in earlier periods of capitalist development. Unevenness of economic development among nations is not only useful for the supranationals, but also a necessary aspect of their business. Beyond the well-known advantages given to such industries as oil in the perpetuation of relatively underdeveloped Third World states in the Middle East and Latin America, differences among "advanced" capitalist countries are equally valuable. Peasants and marginal workers of the least advanced countries become sources of cheap labor to fill the expansion needs of the most developed nations. Algerians are to be found in French factories, or Turks in German industry; many Italians who migrated to West Germany have recently been shipped back home because of stagnation of the West German economy. Even in the Eastern bloc the same phenomenon

---

* I employ the term "supranational" in order to denote corporations whose operations are relatively independent of the constraints of nation states. "Multinational" is a descriptive term for certain corporations that transcend national boundaries and includes capital that has more than one "national" identity.

obtains: Polish "guest workers" are to be found in East Germany.

Relative unevenness in development also produces favorable conditions for capital investment by both the supranationals and sections of national capital. Thus, rather than risk the political consequences of an international working class sharing equal working and living conditions, the supranationals prefer to maintain the differential wage rates, living standards and working conditions. To be sure, the maintenance of nation states creates serious difficulties for the large corporations doing their business on a world scale. But the advantages outweigh the problems for the time being, even though it means that "crisis" becomes the most descriptive category of contemporary capitalism.

As I have noted, the food industry is also an international industry. In the nineteenth century, much of the capital for the development of the great manufacturing industries was accumulated by the export of agricultural products. Farm interests have fought the large corporations over the division of the agricultural pie. High transportation rates, processors' profits, and the growth of powerful food retailing chains have cut deeply into the income of working as well as corporate farms. Food growers have always fought the railroads, the "middlemen" and the banks that often controlled intermediate businesses. But the farmers never won their battle for a larger share of the retail price of food. Instead processors and the government offered another way out—overseas markets. As long as farmers accepted expanded markets, and the corporations and government needed a way out of the dilemmas of international business, a marriage of convenience could be effected.

Contrary to the popular belief that farmers were resolute opponents of the growth of corporate power, even the yeoman farmer eventually became convinced that American imperial expansion was really in his interest. The populist movement against railroads and the so-called middlemen who used their monopolistic position to squeeze the small farmers was a significant political development in American history. In the 1870s and 1880s many farmers were persuaded that their economic destiny was antagonistic to the interests of the large trusts which were establishing their domination over transportation and the marketing of food and cotton. But even as agrarian radicalism was waging a powerful, but ultimately rear-guard action against the trusts, strong forces were forging an alliance with the same hated giants. Expansion had ceased within the borders of the United States. Now ideologists of world expansion such as John Fiske and Admiral Mahan were witnessing their theories transformed into the everyday practice of American diplomacy. The enunciation of the Open Door to China and other potential markets by McKinley's Secretary of State John Hay was only the epitome of a policy of capital and commodity export that had characterized the thrust of United States diplomacy since the Mexican War. If the United States had determined to limit its colonial possessions, this decision in no way meant that American imperial ambition had been forsaken.

The transformation of large segments of the agrarian movement from opponents into supporters of the imperial aims of United States corporations was signaled by the careers of Tom Watson of Georgia and Ben Tillman of Alabama, both early and fervent advocates of government regulation of railroads and food processing. These talented legislators became bellicose jingoists in the first decade of the twentieth century as they abandoned their third party movements and returned to the Democratic Party, then under the leadership of William Jennings Bryan. Bryan was later to become an outspoken expansionist as a powerful spokesman for agrarian interests during his tenure as Woodrow Wilson's Secretary of State.

The coalition between financial and agricultural businesses was cemented firmly as the small farmer gave way to the corporate farm in the years after World War I. Factories in the field, owned and often controlled by large banks and insurance companies, became integrated within the larger corporate nexus that pressed for new capital and commodities markets overseas.

Thus it is no exaggeration to claim that the export of agricultural products has been a significant component of favorable United States trade balances throughout this century. American industry not only gathered its initial strength from the productive farm sector, but has relied upon it for currency stability and, to a lesser extent, for the extension of its world political influence. Thus, food is much more than the material substratum of industrial development, insofar as cheap prices ensure relatively low wages and high profit rates that can be translated into investments in new manufacturing industries. Agriculture has become a vital component of foreign economic policy and an extraordinary political weapon to sustain a favorable atmosphere for United States investments in poor nations.

The fundamental reason for the sudden jump in food prices was that agricultural surpluses and basic stocks were pressed into service when the value of the dollar slipped in the late 1960s and began to tumble rapidly in the first two years of this decade. The dollar became weaker because Europe and Japan began to make demands on United States gold reserves. The dollars accumulated in foreign banks to pay for imports, capital exports, the income spent by soldiers and civilians abroad during the Vietnam war and burgeoning tourist trade of the late 1960s, were no longer as valuable as in the "golden" years of the early postwar period. It was vital for the value of United States capital and to prevent a runaway inflation that the United States hold the line on its dwindling gold reserves.

The options available to policy-makers in the federal government and the corporations were severely limited. Even if the Vietnam war could be ended, thereby halting somewhat the flow of dollars abroad, there was no doubt that a United States presence in Southeast Asia was required to protect the six billions of invested capital in oil exploration, mining and other industries in this area. Moreover, the strategic interests of the United States in the entire area were at stake. At the same time, Europeans were reluctant to permit a wholesale withdrawal of U.S. military forces from the North Atlantic Treaty Organization (another source of the dollar and gold drain) because it would mean that European troops would have to replace the United States force. This decision would put new strains on the economies of NATO countries, already beset by inflationary pressures and capital shortages.

Another possibility was equally foreclosed. The United States government, closely allied with the multinational corporations and indeed often interchangeable with them in crucial ways, was simply in no position to order a halt to the flow of U.S. capital abroad. Even though relatively small sums of U.S. capital were large enough to mobilize much larger amounts of European resources under its direction, the volume of United States investments in Europe as well as the developing sections of the world were accelerating in the 1950s and 1960s. It did not matter that capital outflows often meant that the basic means of production within the United States itself were destined to become relatively backward compared to ostensible "competitors" such as Japan, France and West Germany. The

new suprastate transcended national boundaries, but it
relied on national governments to smooth its operation
and to pick up the pieces created by the experiments in international economics.

In the late 1960s our government launched a campaign
against tourism abroad, and announced a devaluation of
the dollar in order to make United States exports more
competitive in price. The devaluation restored the trade
balance in 1970, but despite these measures and the imposition of import duties on certain products, the relative
price of the dollar slipped and gold prices began their
steep rise during 1971-1972.

Once again, the old standby, agriculture, was recruited
to fill the breach. Farm businesses, long restive about
the serious decline of their share of the consumer dollar,
put powerful pressure on the Administration to move
swiftly to ensure a high rate of return on their investments. The price of machinery was higher, the power of
the processors, the wholesalers and retailers was growing,
and Congress was threatening to remove price supports
after nearly forty years of artificially inflated prices.

Added to the thirty-three million acres already retired
from cultivation by long-range "conservation" policies by
1949,[6] Secretary of Agriculture Earl Butz ordered the retirement of another sixty million acres of grain-producing
land in 1971.* Even with more than ninety million acres of
land withdrawn from cultivation, the 1972 crops reached a
record high. In addition, the government was shelling out
more than twenty million dollars a year to store unused
grain. Moreover, a serious surplus of supplies was preventing farm prices from rising to a level high enough to offset
the higher costs of machinery, fertilizer and other factors
of production.

---

* Between 1973 and 1974 some six to seven million acres were put
back into cultivation by the Agriculture Department.

Rising demands for finding markets abroad coincided with the Soviet offer. If the Soviets and other "hungry" buyers could drain off enough wheat, corn and soybeans, not only would prices rise on the world market but also on the domestic market where three-quarters of the crops were ordinarily consumed. With government help in negotiations as well as price supports, a price was established that the Soviets were delighted to accept. The deal was worth more than one billion dollars and went a long way toward reestablishing the trade balances that had slipped badly in 1972. The dollar began to revive during the following year, even though gold prices kept rising. Together with a second devaluation, which placed both agricultural and manufactured goods in an extremely favorable position against foreign imports, exports took a broad jump and United States corporate investments were saved.

The Soviet Wheat Deal was a key element in the maturation of the détente between the United States and the Soviet Union that has become a keystone of U.S. diplomacy. Apart from the role played by the deal in helping to restore the U.S. balance of payments, it can be understood in terms of a quid pro quo of international relations. The Soviets were helped to solve their own farm crisis by the wheat deal. In return, their efforts in Vietnam assisted the United States to make a graceful exit, and they secured U.S. capital for the development of natural gas in Siberia.

However, the solution abroad introduced new problems at home. Livestock raisers found the prices of feed prohibitive. It became cheaper to slaughter cattle and poultry early and use them for feed, rather than wait until they were ready for market. The price controls of President Nixon's "Phase 3" economic policy pushed against spiraling production costs. In effect, the cattle growers went on strike, refusing to submit beef, poultry and pork stocks at the prevailing price. When controls were lifted in spring 1973, meat prices went sky-high and a boycott was instituted by angry consumers faced with less supply and variety that were offered at nearly twice the 1967 prices and at as much as 50 percent more than prices established by the controls program. Prices of cheaper cuts of beef, those bought by working class people, rose even higher than the expensive cuts. Between 1967 and September, 1973, the consumer food price index rose by 48.3 percent, and eggs, poultry, fish and many other commodities were much higher.

In the wake of the inflationary spurt, Secretary Butz ordered three million acres of arable land to be placed under cultivation again, but food prices failed to sink to "normal," now defined as "only" 4 percent above the previous year's level. By the fall, the price of wheat had soared to $5 a bushel, three times the price just fifteen months earlier. By January 1974 the baking industry and government officials were predicting that bread would be sold at $1 a pound at the retail stores. Nor was there any indication that meat, poultry or dairy products were destined for immediate reductions, even though none of them seemed to be in short supply. Paradoxically, even though the higher prices of grains and livestock did solve the "shortages," the laws of supply and demand were not controlling price levels. The restoration of larger quantities of all kinds of food after the temporary drain generated by increased exports did not reflect itself in domestic prices. In fact, food prices continued their apparently inexorable climb during the winter of 1974.

II

The steep price rises during 1973 were an unusual episode magnifying a long-term trend. Since 1959 food prices had risen by nearly 65 percent even before the sensational increases of 1973 and 1974. At the same time the food growers' share of the retail dollar diminished from more than half to about 35 percent. The postwar period was a time of consolidation for all sectors of the food industry. Competition between growers and processors, wholesalers and retailers, intensified in the 1950s and within the farm sector itself, leading to an unprecedented era of mergers and combinations.

The major trend in farming during this period was toward the consolidation of ownership in fewer hands. Since the end of the Depression, this movement has been continual. The number of farms has shrunk to the point that by 1973, it was estimated, only 2.5 million farms remained and less than 1.5 million of these were full-time commercial enterprises. Even more important, less than 2 percent of them accounted for one-third of all sales. In 1970 smaller farms, those earning $10,000 a year or less, accounted for less than 10 percent of sales, while farms earning $40,000 a year or more obtained 56 percent of the market in 1971. Considering the fact that many of the smaller farms were worked by part-time owner-operators, the number of full-time farms was only slightly more than one million by 1974, and those were dominated by corporations.[7]

By the first years of the 1970s many of the largest farms were owned or controlled by food processors. Key processor-farm owners such as Del Monte, Libby Foods and Seabrook Farms dominated fruit and vegetable production in the United States. These and other corporations controlled 85 percent of retail vegetable sales and 69 percent of food and nut sales in 1969, indicating the emergence of what is called "vertical integration" as the characteristic feature of the food industry since 1960.[8] Behind companies such as Hunt and Foremost as well as Del

Monte, conglomerates such as Tenneco, Kaiser, Greyhound and ITT were beginning to use their huge stores of capital, gouged from defense contracts, to enter the agribusiness. Agriculture was among the major sources of investments for the Bank of America and most major California farms were either owned or controlled by the Bank or conglomerates by the 1960s. The degree of concentration achieved by these corporations is staggering. The control over farms by relatively few large processors, which in turn are dominated by banks and large holding companies, means that price fixing in agriculture has become as feasible as in the auto and steel industries.

Just as officials of the Commerce Department have been interchangeable with officials of large corporations since the early 1900s, so has the Agriculture Department followed the same course. Secretary of Agriculture Earl Butz was a former official of the Ralston-Purina Company, a big grain processor. The Assistant Secretary, Robert Long, was with the Bank of America. These Nixon appointments ensure the cooperation of the government in the task of bringing agriculture under the aegis of corporate capital.

Edward Higbee's statement that "farming has become a high-speed business rather than a way of life" [9] is not only illustrated by the tendency toward concentration of ownership or the rapid mechanization of agriculture, but also by the powerful support the government has given to help create the conditions that enable the largest corporations to increase their share of farm production. Government price-support policies are oriented toward the largest growers who have accumulated millions of dollars in price supports. In 1959 Senator John Williams (R. Del.) estimated that the three largest farm corporations received more price-support money from the Federal Government than the states of Pennsylvania, New Jersey, Delaware and Maryland combined[10]; 56 percent of the farms received less than 7 percent of all supports.

Subsidies to retire farmlands, for bolstering profits in the face of low export prices, for storage of surpluses, and in the form of low-cost, government-sponsored electrification, research and pest-control projects, have combined to facilitate higher profits for the largest growers. These profits are invested in purchases of more lands from marginal farmers, used to diversify investments in processing and retailing and in the further mechanization of farming itself. In essence, government assistance programs have strengthened the monopolistic power of the largest firms.

Millions of small farmers were forced into the cities despite the myth that the agricultural policies of the New Deal and successive administrations were oriented to preserving the competitive basis of agriculture by helping the small grower to stay in business. Others hang on in the countryside, eking out a marginal living by subcontracts to the big growers who determine the price of the small farmers' produce. The existence of a relatively large number of small farms sustains the myth that they are not mean agricultural laborers but are the historical successor to the yeoman around which the American myth of competitive enterprise is fashioned. But hundreds of thousands of small farmers have lost contact with the "free" market. Their whole harvest is committed to a single large processor or wholesaler even prior to the planting. Farming on contract places the small farmer at the mercy of the large corporation and really makes many farmers, even those who employ farm laborers, little more than managers or workers for absentee owners.

Thus mechanization on the farms and processing plants has meant that labor costs as a share of sales have declined, refuting the argument that high food prices are the result of higher wages. The wage-cost push theory applies least of all to the food industry compared to other sectors where the argument appears, at least on the surface, to be more plausible. Productivity per labor hour has consistently exceeded wage increases for more than twenty years. The farm laborer, among the lowest paid of all industrial workers, is also among the least unionized. As a result, farm wages as a percentage of sale prices are extremely low in comparison to the rest of American industry. For example, wages are 4 percent of the retail price of non-union lettuce, a target of the National Farmworkers Union's organizing efforts in the past several years. Fulltime farm workers earned only $3,170 a year, while partly employed workers, comprising 87 percent of all farm workers, earned a miserable $1,160 a year in 1971.[11]

The situation is better among food-processing workers. In the processing sector, about one-third of the workers are unionized. The average wage was $155 a week in 1970, but much of this work is seasonal. The weekly wage includes overtime of as much as ten hours, so the hourly and yearly income of processing workers is often just over $100 a week, or $2.50 an hour, which is about a dollar an hour less than the average industrial wage for that year.

Wages for workers employed by retail food chains and the so-called "independents" are also far below those of other unskilled and semiskilled workers in unionized manufacturing industries. The less than $3 an hour average wage in 1973 for such job categories as checkers, produce-men, and general workers in these stores contrasts with wages of $5 an hour in automobile assembly plants, and similar levels in chemicals, rubber, oil and other basic industries. With an industry less than 15 percent unionized in 1973, and a large number of part-time workers in many categories, it is hardly surprising that wage levels are well below those in manufacturing industries.[12]

Clearly neither the labor costs in the farm sector, the processing sector, nor retailing can match the influence of the growth of large, vertically integrated corporations as important factors in determining the rising cost of food. But among the most important points to be remembered about the rising price of processed food is that for the first time profits in this sector are matching profits in traditionally more lucrative industrial and commercial enterprises. The tendency toward a high degree of concentration of ownership and control in all branches of the food industry, including the trend toward vertical integration, means that investment decisions for agricultural expansion are made on the same basis as in any other industry. The sources of large investments are the banks, the large retail chains and food processors, and some of the internally financed agricultural combines. These corporations found intolerable the relatively low rates of profits in food that prevailed before World War II. It was only through measures to control larger shares of the market at all levels of the food industry that the leading corporations interested in expansion could ensure profit rates that were sufficient to justify their investment. Having reached their objectives in terms of production and distribution control, the large vertically integrated corporations that mainly grew out of the retail side and the processing side made their move on the price front during 1970-1973.

III

As early as 1967, economist Ben Seligman, formerly research director of the Retail Clerks International Association, advanced the point of view that monopoly control over retailing, especially the growth of supermarket chains and involuntary "independent" grocery coöperative buying arrangements, was driving prices upward.[13] Seligman raised the question of the developing vertical integration between the wholesaler and the retailer, using The Great Atlantic & Pacific Tea Company (A & P) as his prototype. By 1948 national and regional chains controlled 35 percent of the food market. By 1963, their control reached 47 percent of retail food sales, while affiliated grocers captured another 44 percent through direct buying from processors and farmers. In 1966, the first large-scale consumer boycott of supermarkets to stem the upward spiral of prices ended in failure, but brought to national attention the significance of the chain stores as a cause of inflation. By 1963 the top four chains controlled half the food sales in 218 metropolitan areas, while the top 8 had 62 percent of these sales. Seligman pointed out that the profit margins of the major chains such as Safeway, A & P, Acme, and Kroger rose by more than 35 percent each, while the increase for the retail food industry as a whole was 28 percent between 1949 and 1965.

Since it is generally agreed by economists studying price movements that 40 percent of market control is usually sufficient for a group of retailers or manufacturers to be able to set prices, it is reasonable to suggest that eight major national retail food chains have effective control over price movements in their sector.

During the period when retail chains were competing with the "mom and pop" grocery stores, there is little question that their lower prices benefited the consumer. This consumer advantage lasted from about 1930, when supermarket chains began operation in earnest, to the early 1960s. As chain-store buying became characteristic of all retail sales, and even "independent" grocers were depending on wholesalers who controlled their buying, the whole concept of competition in food retailing has become no more than a faint memory. Small grocers are almost exclusively used by ordinary shoppers for Sunday or late-night buying. On the West Coast and in an increasing number of other market areas, twenty-four-hour supermarkets are squeezing out the remaining small grocers.

The number of items offered for sale on supermarket shelves has proliferated in the past decade. Even though profits on investments are about equal to those earned by other large businesses, the huge volume of food sales which accrued to the big chains, estimated in 1973 to be more than $150 billion, helps to make the volume of profits extremely large.

Control by the national and regional chains over food retailing has made them extremely powerful in their relations with processors and agribusinesses. As I have noted, ownership of disparate functions in the food business is not the only means of achieving vertical integration. Sometimes the retail chains control all aspects of the food industry through the device of the exclusive contract, which subordinates other aspects of the industry to its rule without direct ownership. Or a large processor, such as Consolidated Foods, will enter the retail chain business and achieve integration through its position as a wholesaler. But the retailers seem to have achieved the most sophisticated level of vertical integration. In 1967 Seligman estimated that some of them were able to supply as much as 65 percent of their own needs through control over processing and contracting out food growing.

Retail prices are jacked up by "gimmicks" such as trading stamps and promotion campaigns for new brands. The trading-stamp hoax is among the most horrendous perpetrated on the consumer. The purchase of stamps appears to be only an inducement to buy in one store instead of another. Yet nearly all retail chains feature stamps as part of their promotion drives. The price of the goods exchanged for the stamps is simply added on to the cost of food, and it has been estimated that, in many cases, recipients of the stamps gain absolutely no benefit from them. At least 12 percent of all stamps issued are never redeemed, even though consumers actually pay for them in higher food prices.

All along the line, from increasing concentration of ownership and control in the agricultural sector, which are buttressed by government policies aimed at enhancing the power of the large agribusinesses, to the virtual elimination of the small food retailer, the structure of the food industry has changed radically. The vision of the sod-buster, small cattle rancher, the "mom and pop" grocery store, so intrinsic to the myth of free enterprise, lacks even the scattered evidence needed to perpetuate it. The monopoly control over the food business is so startling because it explodes the powerful images of social and characterological independence which sustains so much of American ideology.

Among the ideological underpinnings of American life, the notion of social mobility remains critical. As recently as the 1950s and 1960s the farm and other types of small independent businesses were a central archetypical image of mobility for millions of newly urbanized persons from the southern and western agricultural regions. Hundreds of thousands remained on the farm despite dwindling incomes; their mortgages were subsidized by factory jobs, which were disdainfully regarded as a necessary evil. The sustaining myth, however, was that one day conditions would permit a return to full-time farming for those who remained, and a return to the countryside for those forced to live in the cities. One need only recall W. R. Burnett's *Asphalt Jungle* and the pitiful journey of the wounded criminal to recapture his lost youth on the farm to understand the significance of this idea.

Black Americans left the land with far more ambivalent feelings than whites. Even though the city offered neither satisfying work nor decent housing, nor for the most part a refuge from the repressiveness of Southern institutions, there was at least the chance to earn a decent income. The black family, which had formed the base of the old sharecropper homestead, at first retained much of its solidity within the ghetto environment and provided some measure of resistance to the disintegrating effects of the urban social environment. Thus, despite much travel to the South, the blacks who had migrated since the 1920s knew that they could not go home again.

As for the native-born whites who entered the factories after being driven from the farm, there were no sustaining institutions to help them attenuate the sense of having been wrenched from their natural habitat. Unlike the blacks and the European immigrants, displaced farmers lacked the distinguishing racial and ethnic traditions that could have maintained a cultural identity. No agrarian organization calling itself Sons of the Soil arose to play the same role of easing the pain of assimilation into the hostile city as the Polish Falcons, the burial societies of a score of nationalities and the black extended family. Yet, until recently at least, the hope of returning to an agrarian life was never far from the consciousness of many white workers.

On the other hand, a peculiar type of agrarian nostalgia gripped a section of the suburban-bred middle class youth of the 1960s who had no rural ancestral roots. Having become disenchanted with the bourgeois lifestyles of their professional and corporate manager parents, these young people sought utopian solutions to the question of how to lead their own lives. The return to open spaces, nonindustrial countryside or agricultural pursuits represented for them the ultimate revolt against their social origins. Of course, many failed to take account of the whole historical movement away from the countryside because of its lack of economic viability for most small farmers. A burst of enthusiasm was subsidized, at first, by family funds. But, in many cases, when confronted by the practical problems of making the farm pay, the long march back to the city became inevitable. For others, especially sons and daughters of eastern and southern European immigrants, social mobility meant not so much the chance to become a doctor or lawyer, although these professions were chosen by a few, but the eventual ownership of a small business, particularly in the sale of food and beverages, which made endurable the protracted hardships of industrial or commercial labor.

Now, not only is the small farm all but extinguished from the American landscape but the small retail store is also becoming just a memory. The general grocery store survives in the ghettos and barrios of large cities and to a diminishing degree in the countryside, but it has become an anachronism almost everywhere else. The traditional youth hangout, the candy store, has yielded in all but isolated places. Candy undergoes the same packaging as toilet paper in the local supermarket. All soft drinks are purchased in bottles or cans. The penny-candy store, once a refuge of old and young city dwellers, has been revived in the middle class pseudo-bohemias as just another profitable business and cultural artifact.

The person possessing what Erich Fromm has called an "independent social character" [14] has no place to turn. Since eight out of nine new business ventures annually end in failure, the prospects are grim indeed for those who manage to scrape together their savings and a bank loan to produce some working capital. Although workers yearning to go it alone and become their own boss have been obliged to occupy the interstices of American business for nearly a century, until now the particular frontier of small businesses was never quite closed. The final victory of the large corporations in food retailing and farming has sounded the death knell for the hopes of millions.

Perhaps the only form in which the mobility myth lives and thrives is in the replacement of the independent small business by the franchise. Even though the small "owner" is little more than a manager of a unit of a large food retailing and processing chain, such national franchise operations as Carvel, Kentucky Fried Chicken and Orange Julius attract those wishing to go into business by offering "investment" opportunities. The prospective proprietor is required to advance a relatively small amount of cash to qualify for the franchise, but must purchase only from the central distribution agency and feature goods entirely determined from above. In some cases, this rigid requirement is relaxed provided a certain quantity is purchased from the distributor. The impetus to enter franchised business in gas retailing as well as food retailing is no different from the conditions that regularly produced many new businesses in the past, the chief difference between the two being that the amount of autonomy afforded the franchised businessman is infinitely smaller than the old coffee shop, ice cream parlor or grocery store. Symbolic of our times, a recent exhibit at the New York Coliseum was centered around franchise opportunities for "small businessmen."

IV

The last issue in this analysis seems so self-evident as to be banal. Yet it is frequently forgotten by those whose propensity is to confine economic calculations to quantitative effects. Much of the rise in food prices is directly attributable to the way in which we live, especially our eating habits.

It is now almost a commonplace to be reminded that eating is as much a part of the culture as rock music. Like rock music, food is both a part of the popular traditions brought here from elsewhere and a manufactured commodity. Unfortunately, the health-food industry, a big business that thrives on the sense of horror many of us experience when we become aware of the fact that the food we buy rarely resembles its natural state, is but an instance of the tendency for all natural functions to be transformed into commodities in our society. In the case of food, the transformations are marvelous from an engineering standpoint and equally hideous from the perspective of culture. In 1973 we consumed a large portion of our potato crop as potato chips. Not only does frying of potatoes effectively remove most of their nutrients, consume huge quantities of oil, and add unhealthy weight to the person, but potato chips are extremely costly as well. While a pound of potatoes in February, 1974, cost about $.20, a pound of potato chips cost as much as $1.40. Such discrepancies are not entirely the result of food processing or the increased costs associated with such additives as chemical preservatives, shortening and salt. Prices climb when packaging becomes a major factor in marketing and when the product is given a brand name and is advertised on billboards, TV and radio and the print media. And many more examples could be cited besides potato chips or food products that have eliminated, in large measure, consumption of natural foods. Almost everything we buy is commercially processed. The function of mass advertising is to transmute desires or wants so that they can only be satisfied by the new synthetic products.

## APPROXIMATE COST OF SAMPLE
## UNPROCESSED AND PROCESSED FOODS
## NEW YORK CITY FEBRUARY, 1974 [15]

| | Unprocessed or Minimal Processing | Canned | Frozen | Frozen Processed | Other Processed |
|---|---|---|---|---|---|
| chicken | 49-59¢/lb. out of season | | | | |
| corn | 25-29¢/lb. | | 35¢/lb. | fried-$1.20/lb. in butter or cream sauce 64¢/lb. | Corn chips 82¢/lb. |
| fish | $1.69-1.75/lb. | | fillets 79¢-$1.15/lb. | breaded fillets-$1.20/lb. fish cakes 89¢/lb. fish sticks $1.38/lb. | |
| onions | 30¢/lb. | boiled 50¢/lb. | chopped 53¢/lb. | fried onion rings 69¢/lb. | |
| potatoes | 20-25¢/lb. | boiled 27¢/lb. | | french fries 37¢/lb. shoestring 48¢/lb. | potato chips $1.30/lb. |
| rice | reg. white 50-55¢/lb. | spanish 32¢/lb. (water added in cooking) | rice-verde cooked w/ peppers & rice 60¢/lb. | | instant 77¢/lb. Ric-a-Roni 88¢/lb. specialty packages $1.60/lb. |
| **Wheat Products** | | | | | |
| bread—store-brand white 36¢/lb. | | Brown 'n Serve white rolls 80¢/lb. | hamburger buns 80¢/lb. | English Muffins 70¢/lb. bread-sticks $1.25/lb. | croutons $1.80/lb. Saltines 51¢/lb. |

As domination by the vertically integrated corporations of the food industry has increased, the needs creation and needs fulfillment cycle becomes more characteristic of food buying. There are few alternatives to processed food for city dwellers whose physical isolation from the sources of raw foods prevents any but the most minimal efforts to overcome the inflationary impact of the processing industries.

Notwithstanding a modest revival in baking in the home over the past several years, bread and cake baking is still a mystery for most urban Americans. Even the so-called home-baked cakes and cookies are drawn from pre-mixed packages. And premixed soups, meats, grain products and even cheeses are found all over supermarket shelves. The recent attempt to soften the high prices asked for meats by allowing beef with "vegetable protein" (meaning soybeans or, worse, artificial mixtures) is just another example of the disappearance of food that is not manufactured.

A major reason for the high prices of food, therefore, is the cultivation of tastes that rely on processing for their satisfaction. Part of the development of these tastes has been the structure of urban life that has persuaded many persons that there "is no time" for cooking, baking and other methods of preparing raw foods. The processes of homogenization are not merely a function of perceived time limitations, however. Chemical additives have permitted the simulation of smoothness, and processing allows convenient packaging and more efficient use of storage spaces.

The notion of convenience, partly an ideology that relates to the almost compulsive avoidance of toil made necessary by the routines of housework such as cleaning and washing, provides much resonance for purchasing packaged foods. But the pressures of time and the blandishments afforded by the doctrine of convenience do not exhaust the reasons why packaged, premixed foods have found a willing market among consumers. Another appeal is to the profound sense of helplessness and incompetence fostered by the culture of specialization and professionalization within industry. Clearly, the individual cannot be trusted to slice his/her own bread because the slices will inevitably be uneven. Sliced bread, introduced by baking companies in the late 1920s, was a prototype of a veritable avalanche of prepackaged products that have appeared on the market since. Advertisements warn housewives that they cannot make decent coffee without premeasured packages. One major coffee brand, owned by General Foods, has developed a "scientific" system of measured portions, packaged in tin foil so that the anxious homemaker will not ruin her husband's business dinner or her prestige with his parents by making coffee that is too strong or too weak. Sexual and love dissatisfaction is hinted at as well because, as everyone knows, a man will not tolerate a mate who makes a bad pot of coffee, and seasoning is much too complicated a task to be entrusted to the fumbling housewife. She needs a "Hamburger Helper" or a breading product that does not risk putting too many bread crumbs on the meat or too few.

Part of the tendency toward programmed eating is probably a reflection of the fact that larger numbers of women are working full- or part-time outside the home than ever before. Their sense of confidence in the kitchen and their ability to manipulate its productive apparatus are no doubt severely diminished. But, the orders from above are not restricted to the issue of whether the person can create their meals. When a coffee processor or a chocolate pudding company wraps individual portions, they are also structuring such questions as how much food it is considered proper to eat. The size of bread slices is not only a question of convenience, it is also an ordering of how much consumers themselves want or need to eat. Images of proper size and weight are not only imposed by fashion, but by the actual structure of retailing. This practice adds to the costs of food.

Children constitute a pressure on adults to purchase certain cereals, brands of "enriched" breads (i.e., those loaves whose nutritional values have been expunged by processing and reconstituted by synthetic vitamins) and such meat alloys as cold cuts. Food processing fits into the whole pattern of socialization in America where the children become pawns in the advertising game and a medium to generate guilt within their parents, or, worse, feelings of impotence against the constant incitement to buy. To the extent that the masses have come to regard acquired manipulated tastes as part of the natural order of things, processed foods and high prices are sustained by consumer demands.

Yet there can be no question of the origin of food processing as a characteristic cultural fact that supports patterns of economic domination over the food supply. Food processing is profitable and the more steps between the farm product and the item that appears on the shelf of the retail store, the more profitable it becomes.

We are undergoing a period of transition in our eating and food-buying habits. Having been prepared to eat chemical additives, processed foods, and alloyed foods, we are about to witness the coming of a new era, the two-class food system. Poor people, workers and those living in retirement and other kinds of fixed incomes will, most probably, be offered a diet of "vitamin enriched" processed foods. These will do away with "pure beef," fresh vegetables, and raw grains. Bargain prices will be offered as an incentive to purchase "near" meat, "near" vegetables and imitation breads and cakes.

It is clear that there are no absolute shortages of key items such as meat, grain and vegetables unless commodities earmarked for foreign trade and processing are discounted. The processes of food production are equally germane to the question of both high prices and food shortages. Finally, government policies were as responsible as any other single factor for generating the long-term conditions that produced inflation and such shortages as appeared at retail counters.

Thus, what would be necessary for the construction of an economy that could provide cheap food commensurate with the enormous productivity of our agriculture is nothing less than a redefinition of the concepts of taste and efficiency as well as a new structure of ownership and control over the food industry and the economy as a whole. A careful examination of the role and development of American agriculture reveals the fact that the question of the food crisis is the same as the crisis of the American economy and its culture.

# 3

# "Seven Sisters" On the Make

---

The concept of overproduction has been the organizing principle of the various energy industries since the end of World War I. Shortages occurred in World War II, but ever since then the United States has seemed cursed with a surfeit of fuels. In fact, the problem for the oil industry, which became the most important source of industrial and home heating fuel, has not been extraction or refining but nearly always marketing. For much of the post-World War II era motorists were tempted by an unending series of gimmicks to persuade them to purchase a particular brand of gasoline rather than its competitors. Free vacations, trading stamps, "special additives" purporting to increase mileage, eliminate "engine knock," or tune the entire engine were, until recently, a persistent feature of American gasoline marketing.

The overproduction of energy really began with the coal industry, which showed a sharp increase in the number of mechanized mines after 1950 while simultaneously suffering an almost complete eclipse as a home heating fuel. After the mid-1950s coal was used almost exclusively for industrial purposes, mainly for the production of electricity and steel. During the offensive of the environmentalists, which reached its apex a decade later, it even looked as if coal might go the way of the transcontinental rail system that once dominated long-distance travel.

The oil industry, too, was said to be in a deep crisis of overproduction in the early 1960s. Refinery capacity was over expanded, and exploration for new sources of oil within the North American continent slowed to a crawl compared to the expansion of Middle Eastern and Latin American sources. But once it had lowered the price of fuel at the retail level to enable it to compete successfully with the coal industry and to discourage the development of nuclear energy, the oil industry found itself under attack on many fronts. Congressional opponents of the industry were taking a hard look at the long-standing oil depletion allowance, which permits oil companies to receive tax exemptions on the first 27.5 percent of their income. Why should taxpayers subsidize oil explorations that were no longer being carried on within the United States? How was the industry contributing to the development of the natural resources of the country if it failed to develop offshore oil and other important supplies? Criticism of the oil industry's performance resulted in a small reduction of the depletion allowance, to 22 percent, in the late 1960s. Although the new law failed to make much of a dent in oil corporate profits, it was a signal that the oil companies had entered a time of trial.

At the same time, Congress resisted the oil industry's request for the construction of a pipeline extending from the Alaska shelf, a rich source of crude oil, to refineries within the United States and Canada. The pipeline, said the growing environmentalist lobby, would result in a serious erosion of Alaska lands, destroy its natural beauty and endanger the migrating wildlife.

I

The energy "shortages" that caused long lines at gas pumps, cold living rooms, sharp rises in fuel prices and the introduction of rationing in many states of the Union is a complex story. Its most remarkable feature has to be the oil companies' success in winning nearly all of their objectives, albeit at the cost of suffering a serious loss of credibility. However, for an industry that has been able to take control of most of the largest coal producers, a growing proportion of the nuclear fuels industry, a substantial share of the chemicals industry dependent upon oil for raw materials, as well as all phases of the oil industry itself—marketing and transportation as much as drilling and refining —popularity is certainly not the major requirement for survival. For even without it, the major oil companies succeeded in thwarting any serious movement toward increased public regulation, much less public ownership, though they held both industrial and private users at their mercy during the worst days of the crisis. Plastics manufacturers, auto companies, steel producers and other major users found their production schedules disrupted. Developing countries in Asia, Africa and Latin America were facing bankruptcy as crude oil prices increased more than 700 percent within a year. Japan and European nations watched their international trade position weaken within a few months.

Yet it would be an error to assume that this exhibition of naked power did not entail serious problems for the largest oil corporations. In the wake of persistent public demand for full disclosure of the facts about oil supplies it became increasingly difficult to maintain the veil of secrecy that ordinarily shrouded their operations.

The proud arrogance of the largest producers was pilloried but by no means destroyed by the deep currents of distrust that ran through the populace. Corporate statistics purporting to show that supplies of crude oil ran well behind rising demand were being questioned. In the face of a 6 to 7 percent annual increase in the use of oil and a commensurate increase in the supply of crude oil, refined oil production in the late months of 1973 was running about 10 percent *below* the level of the previous year.

Perhaps the most frustrating aspect of the crisis was the revelation that all information about the oil industry was supplied by its own sources. The government had no independent information, nor did anyone else. And so the battle for information became an important factor in determining public attitudes toward the oil companies. The more homeowners and motorists suffered the effects of the shortages, the less plausible became oil company explanations for the shortages and their arguments for price increases to provide incentives for new drilling.

The first reasons for doubt were provided by the government itself, which disputed industry estimates of the extent of the actual shortages. Nor were many Americans inclined to give credence to Arco's President Thomas Bradshaw,[1] who proclaimed that "We've got to get used to living in a situation where we are short of all forms of energy." The sudden reversal by the industry of its posture of plenitude was too difficult to assimilate in the light of history.

It was not only the contradictory reports from various "authoritative sources" about the extent of the shortages that challenged the credibility of those who swore that the shortages were "real." Newspaper stories revealed that different regions of the country were receiving varying allocations of the now-precious fuel. For example, Ohio was said to be swimming in the stuff, while the oil-parched northeastern states experienced real hardships. Media pundits such as Howard K. Smith celebrated the event as a boon to habits of "discipline" that had been seriously eroded during the affluent sixties, and Lyndon Johnson's former Secretary of the Interior, Stewart Udall, toured the country assuring one and all that the energy crisis was a blessing in disguise because it would force attention to the demands of the conservationists. Udall exhorted his listeners to help reverse the historical level of material culture and asked that they introduce a new ethic into national life:

> "An end to wastefulness, the practice of thrift, is always good for the individual and the nation. If we have to trim down, slim down, tighten our belts a little more—who knows? It may be that our society will be a happier, healthier place, and we'll all live richer lives." Udall urged his fellow Americans to "think small . . . Go lean. Think slow. We've got to cut back. We've got to conserve." [2]

It was plain that Americans were being prepared to accept crisis as a regular feature of their daily existence. The early statements of corporate leaders and neo-liberals of the environmental movements now sounded remarkably alike. Each urged adjustment to, rather than protests against, the shortages. Although corporate statements never mentioned the old bourgeois values Udall had enunciated, the liberals were quick to evoke images reminiscent of Wesley, Calvin and Luther. The energy shortage signaled the revival of quietism as a philosophy of life.

But many Americans were no longer willing to respond

to the offensive of neo-Calvinism with anything but contempt. The Watergate affair of the same year, the food inflation combined with the energy shortage, made all appeals to the doctrine of sacrifice anathema. The new ideology of scarcity was simply too unbelievable to be embraced without proof of a clear and present danger to the national security. In January, 1974, the first manifestations of consumer anger were felt as fights broke out at gas stations when station owners attempted to halt sales or when motorists attempted to circumvent their turn on line. Nearly 200 bombings of gas stations were reported, while gas-tank locks became a scarce commodity.

Some observers noted the relationship between scarcity and the behavior of humans as "naked apes." The manifestations of sharp competitiveness, disciplined waiting in gas lines, the return of careful planning of the day to allow sufficient time to get gas, all attested to the fact that discipline was, indeed, connected to accumulation and deprivation.

As fuel prices rose, considerable agitation became noticeable among those who made their living transporting goods in vehicles with internal-combustion engines. Although the increases in gas prices ripped deeply into the real wages of working people, small truckers seemed the hardest hit because the price of fuel affected their incomes more directly. In any case, the first mass actions took place in January among the "owner-operators" who protested the higher diesel fuel prices and the reductions in the speed limits on interstate highways ordered by President Nixon's administration. Slower trucking speeds meant that it would take longer to reach transport destinations. Truckers would be forced to carry fewer loads each week and profits would be reduced.

Bypassing normal avenues of redress, the truck operators chose a direct method to express their fury at the seemingly discriminatory policies of the oil companies and the government. They simply began to block highways with their trucks, forcing a swift response from the federal energy office, whose willingness to negotiate at first failed to persuade truckers to return to normal runs. At the Delaware Water Gap in southern New Jersey, National Guard units were mobilized to clear the highway by force. Truckers took to the hills and drove the Guard back with a flurry of rifle fire. Similar incidents occurred on the Pennsylvania and Ohio turnpikes as the situation escalated into a small guerrilla war. Finally, owing largely to the intervention of Governor Milton J. Shapp of Pennsylvania, the federal government was obliged to offer some concessions to the rebels. But the extent of the offer was unsatisfactory to them. A 6 percent hike in freight rates was all that the Interstate Commerce Commission permitted, although higher fuel prices and lower speed limits—according to the truckers—were cutting their income by at least 15 percent.

For a time the protests continued. The truckers hoped to be able to force further concessions. Soon they were joined by working truck drivers, part of whose income depended on their ability to travel the highways with dispatch. But the administration was intransigent. It understood well the consequences of bowing too deeply to mass protests. Even if the truckers could be placated with a few more upward adjustments, their example of direct action might engender outbursts from other sectors, particularly motorists whose "cooperation" was relied upon to allow prices to rise with a minimum of political and social acrimony.

Moreover, the administration was concerned that trade union demands for nearly ten million workers whose contracts were scheduled to expire in 1974 would reflect the higher food and fuel prices. The truckers' actions could only exacerbate militancy. Clearly, any exhibition of softness in the face of truckers' demands would jeopardize the administration's hold-the-line wage policy.

One serious effect of the oil crisis was the slowly rising rate of joblessness that accompanied restrictions on oil and coal consumption by industries using large quantities of the fuels. It was more than a question of finding enough fuel to heat industrial plants and offices. The most important impact of fuel shortages and allocation policies was on those manufacturers that used coal and oil as raw materials for the fabrication of products. In early February, 1974, the Bethlehem Steel Corporation announced that it was banking one of its huge furnaces because of the lack of coke needed to produce metals. (The coke shortage was an indirect result of the gasoline shortage— miners went on strike because they claimed they did not receive sufficient gasoline to be able to commute between their homes and the pits.) The reduction in the company's production would reduce its output by one million tons a year. Plastics and other chemical producers using oil as a base material for a wide range of products, too, were fearful that reduced supplies would result in lower production and employment.

What is important for our purposes here is not whether increased layoffs were due to energy shortages or resulted from the slowdown in the economy that was caused by other factors—but that the two phenomena were connected in the public mind, especially as business corporations announced that they would be forced to curtail expansion plans or even regular production schedules because of the shortage of oil or other fuels.

A surprising aspect of the oil shortage was the rising price of coal and the tremendous spurt in coal production brought on, in part, by the crisis. From a position of rapid deterioration in the 1950s and early 1960s, the coal industry seemed to revive miraculously even before the oil crisis became apparent. When it was learned that oil companies had been busily engaged in buying coal companies in the late 1960s, some observers even theorized that the oil shortages were engineered for the specific purpose of promoting coal as a major "new" energy resource to replace the dwindling supplies of both crude and refined oil. Indeed, this theory was given weight by the long-awaited energy report of the panel President Nixon set up to establish a national energy policy. The report emphasized the importance of coal as a replacement for oil, a regression from the hopes generated by the discovery of other forms of energy such as solar, geothermal and fusion power that, only a few years earlier, were expected to render coal obsolete.

Yet, despite the contradictory evidence pointing to a simultaneous shortage of refined oil at the retail level and the plenitude of crude oil in the harbors and storage tanks it would be too simplistic to argue that the so-called energy crisis is a mere ruse. The incontrovertible shortage of United States refining capacity relative to the international and domestic demands for heating fuel and gasoline must be explained. At the same time, it is beyond question that domestic crude oil supplies are inadequate to meet the current requirements of both American industry and the retail demand. For the past thirty years, the United States has relied chiefly on Canadian and Latin American sources of crude oil to meet increasing domestic requirements and has become less dependent on its internal supplies, which really have been rapidly dwindling.

Nevertheless, the immediate catalyst that presumably triggered the shortages—the announcement by Arab nations that they were instituting a boycott against shipments to the United States in the wake of apparent

U.S. support for the Israelis during the latest outburst of fighting in fall 1973—was proven not to be a source of immediate deprivation. The Arabs, it turned out, only accounted for about 7 percent of all crude oil consumed by the United States in 1973. The deprivation of shipments could not have produced such swift results in fall 1973, when gas stations began to close on Sundays and queues appeared wherever gasoline was still for sale. Moreover, when the Shah of Iran announced over national television in February 1974 that shipments had not, in fact, been reduced notwithstanding the alleged boycott during the six-month period ending January, the attempt by the oil companies and the government to pin the whole crisis on the Mideast situation appeared to be headed for complete collapse.

The Shah's statement on the CBS's "60 Minutes" show even went so far as to explain the fate of the missing crude oil shipments. If they were not finding their way to U.S. refineries, where were they going? United States companies were diverting ships to European and Japanese harbors where price controls did not govern or into storage tanks and ships within U.S. ports, awaiting either the end of controls or, more likely, government-controlled price increases.

In 1974, the United States still provided the lion's share of its own needs. By 1975, however, the quantity of crude imports is expected to amount to nearly 40 percent of all supplies and it will probably reach half of all supplies by 1980. This is the heart of the matter. If the United States cannot find internal sources of oil, now our major energy resource, it will either be required to seek alternative sources of energy or it will have to find new ways to get crude oil from its mountains, ocean areas, and other natural resources; that is, unless the Middle East can be assured as a secure supplier.

The Arab oil boycott, however, raised the specter that these reliable foreign supplies of crude oil might be withdrawn from the United States. Since the Eastern hemisphere, primarily the Middle Eastern countries, accounts for 63 percent of the world's known oil reserves, it figures prominently in the future of all industrial countries and may determine the ability of developing countries to achieve their industrial and agricultural objectives. After all, crude oil is one of the major raw materials in the production of fertilizer, an important factor in agricultural productivity. Even though the United States is in a much better position to remain somewhat independent of Middle Eastern crude oil (as for example compared to Japan, which received 97 percent of its oil from this source) the major oil companies that exercised considerable control over Middle Eastern oil production and reserves had reason to be upset by recent events.

For several years the major oil companies have faced much stiffer negotiations with the Middle Eastern oil-producing countries. The majors retained 75 percent ownership as a result of an agreement reached in January, 1973, but are scheduled to relinquish their control by 1982 when the producer countries will assume 51 percent of ownership, leaving the multinational corporations with the remaining 49 percent.

Did the October war signal an effort by the Arabs to abrogate that agreement? Were the oil companies destined to be pushed out of the area much sooner than anticipated? These questions became the basis for extensive trips by both the government's negotiator, Henry Kissinger, and the industry's leader, David Rockefeller, who together assumed direction of the new price agreements in fall 1973.

According to the New York *Daily News* of January 27, 1974, the Administration secretly gave the oil industry broad antitrust exemptions in 1970 so that it could form a solid united front against the Arab threat to nationalize the companies. The oil companies seized this opportunity and successfully staved off the immediate threat of expropriation in the 1972-1973 negotiations.

Two giant supranational corporations, the Aramco Corporation and the Anglo-Iranian oil corporation have owned and controlled the greatest share of Middle Eastern oil fields and oil refineries for many years. For the most part, these corporations have been obliged to share only a small proportion of their profits with Arab countries—in the form of royalty payments on each barrel of crude oil produced. These royalties, which are discounted from the amount of taxes oil companies have to pay to the United States government, provide a substantial quantity of income to Arab governments, but represent only a minuscule proportion of the actual profits of the corporations. For many years Arab leaders have been rankled by this fact. Periodically, they have been successful in negotiating somewhat higher royalty shares with the big four oil companies who constitute the Aramco oil monopoly. This combine of Exxon, Mobil, Standard of California and Texaco (three of Aramco's four shareholders are of Standard Oil origin) has been more than willing to accede to Arab demands for more royalties, but under two conditions: one, the Arabs would make no move toward expropriating the properties of these companies and, two, the large international oil corporations would retain control of the world petroleum market, so that increased royalty payments could be offset by higher prices.

Speculation about the convergence of the October war and the oil shortages of 1973 yields surprising results: first, the Arab offensive was only incidentally directed against Israel. The real target was the United States oil monopolies. It may be argued that the war was an extension of a negotiating strategy of the Organization of Petroleum Exporting Countries (OPEC) to raise royalty payments, procure long-term grants and loans for economic development and some marketing concessions. The issue of nationalization was only a talking point in the conflict. Libya played the role of "bad guy," making threats of imminent expropriation, while Saudi Arabia maintained its friendly and conciliatory posture toward the United States. The Arabs never intended to throw out the corporations from the area. Their interests were entirely directed toward finding a basis for ultimate financial and political accommodation with the two oil monopolies.

So it was not too surprising when Jack Anderson, the nationally syndicated columnist, charged in January 1974, that there was "evidence that the giant U.S. oil combine Aramco encouraged Saudi Arabia to increase oil prices." The increase in crude oil prices in 1973 of 470 percent, widely attributed to Arab demands for higher royalty payments, was believed to be responsible for the higher oil prices that began to be felt at the retail level in the fall of that year. Once again, the facts stand in the way of easy explanations. The problem with ascribing the increases in domestic fuel and gas prices to the Middle Eastern oil-producing countries' demands on the supranationals is that there is considerable room for maneuver that would affect U.S. prices only marginally.

The Middle East has the most productive oil wells in the world. While a United States well yields an average of 18 barrels a day, and Canadian wells produce 200 barrels, Saudi Arabian wells yield 10,117 barrels and Iranian wells produce 15,479 barrels per well each day. The difference in cost of production between Arab and United States crude oil is equally remarkable. In 1969 Michael Tanzer estimated that the cost of a barrel of crude produced in the Middle Eastern countries averaged 10 to 20 cents, while the cost in the United States for a barrel was $1.50.[3] In Venezuela the cost of operating a well was 30 cents a day. In 1969, the world market price of crude oil was $1.50 a barrel—the average costs of production on a world scale were about 25 cents per barrel.

By 1973, at the beginning of the boycott, the price of crude had risen to just under $2 a barrel. But the boycott became the occasion to raise prices by nearly half to $2.85 a barrel. Oil company profits, which had been about 35 cents a barrel, soared to 80 cents a barrel even after royalty payments and taxes were paid. The difference in unit profits of oil produced an additional profit of about $1.35 million a day. By September, 1973, after the Arabs renegotiated with the oil companies, crude prices from Saudi Arabia had soared to around $4.35 a barrel, higher than United States crude prices. The reason for the rise was not only higher royalty payments, but the lifting of import controls by the U.S. government, which allowed Arab oil to be sold within the United States to offset crude oil shortages.

By the end of 1973 foreign crude oil prices had climbed to $9.50 a barrel, almost 50 percent higher than domestic prices. The chief beneficiaries of the price increases were not the Arabs, but the multinationals that controlled 75 percent of the production.

This means that if royalties on Middle Eastern oil rose by 500 percent to raise costs of production, the gap between the world market price and actual costs would be even more immense at present retail price levels.[4] Expropriation would have told an entirely different story, because it would have eliminated the control by the giant monopolies over the sources of crude oil. But this issue was not at the core of the price rises of petroleum on the world market, although it seemed to be a crucial factor determining United States energy policy after 1973. The administration's decision to allow new price rises to the oil companies in order to encourage exploration for new sources of oil on the American continent, experiments to develop other sources of energy besides oil, and the emphasis placed by the government on coal development as a replacement for oil was offered as a way to make the United States self-sufficient in terms of energy resources.

There can be no doubt that the concept of self-sufficiency was invoked as a direct result of the October war. It was the war that justified the revival of coal, the relaxation of environmental protections and the rising price of all types of energy. The war also served as the Administration's reason for encouraging the development of internal sources of oil and other fuels. But the issues were not generated by the war. The war served to make them questions for public debate and action.

There are two other major explanations that are equally important in accounting for oil price rises: first, the quantity of refined oil has actually been declining in the past several years, despite relatively ample provisions for crude oil to the United States from all of its sources; second, and equally important, is the allegation made in the report of Senator Henry M. Jackson's investigating committee's finding that the reasons for the "shortages" and subsequent price rises are mainly related to the drive of the major oil companies, which control 70 percent of domestic production and marketing of crude and refined oil, to take over the remaining 30 percent currently controlled by the so-called independent refiners and marketers. The Federal Trade Commission report, upon which the Jackson findings are based, found that the crucial issue is whether or not the independents shall be permitted by the seven largest oil corporations to receive their share of crude in order to retain their markets.

According to this view, the shortages of crude oil were generated by the large oil companies to starve the refineries and marketing facilities of the independents so as to make them vulnerable for takeovers. The intention of the largest world oil monopolies—Exxon, Royal Dutch Shell, Texaco, Gulf, Standard of California, British Petroleum and Mobil, which control 75 percent of "free world" crude oil production—was to achieve vertical integration to a greater extent than ever before. The crude oil monopoly of the "seven sisters" would facilitate a similar monopoly over refining, distribution and marketing. By making crude supplies "unreliable" and expensive the big companies would be able to squeeze out independent refiners and marketing chains. The higher crude prices offered to refiners would have to be passed on to consumers if the independents were to survive. Yet for much of 1973, government price control policies limited the extent of gas increases. Many independents argued that price control at the retail and wholesale level, while the price of crude oil was allowed to rise unabated, did not so much benefit the consumer as hurt the independents' refining and marketing operations. Apart from Shell, which inexplicably registered a profit loss of 2 percent during the last quarter of 1973 over the same quarter of 1972, each of the Seven Sisters reported increases in earnings for this same period of over 50 percent. Some sample industry profit increases:

Gulf     153%
Getty    115%
Mobil    68%
Standard of Cal.    94%
Texaco   70%
Gen'l Amer. Oil    156%
Occidental Petroleum    272%
Phillips Petroleum    127%
Amer. Petrofina    218% (oil exploration)

The oil industry as a whole reported an average of 80 percent profit increase—as against an average increase in sales of 27 percent. Not surprisingly, profit increases for the first quarter of 1974—which reflect the substantial price hikes won by the oil companies—were even higher.

At the same time, government import policies limited the quantity of both crude and refined oil that could be drawn on for domestic consumption. These restrictions, it was argued, could only result in making crude supplies even more scarce, especially in view of the Arab "boycott." Since nearly all domestic crude oil was appropriated directly by the largest corporations, and the supplies were relatively limited in any case, only a liberal import program could guarantee the survival of the smaller producers. This program was only permitted in May, 1973, after import prices were rising rapidly.

Here it is appropriate to enter a speculation that can be supported by events. Suppose Jack Anderson is right in his claim that the Aramco companies (and the BP-controlled Anglo Iranian Oil Company) were actually encouraging Arab militancy, including the threat of the boycott, and the concomitant rise in the price of crude oil. One reason for this conspiracy might be the curtailment of crude oil imports for the independents. Since independents, particularly marketers, receive more than 50 percent of their requirements from the majors, any limitation in oil supplies at the level of crude or refined oil would place a severe burden on their capacity to survive. The so-called Middle Eastern oil crisis could be related to the attempt of the major seven oil companies, which now control nearly 60 percent of refining capacity (the top twenty control 86 percent), and more than 60 percent of the retail outlets, to extend their control even further.

Only if one understands the process of oil production does this contention become clear. Plentiful supplies of crude oil at competitive prices from other countries are important for the survival of independent refiners and marketers. Yet, despite the relatively low cost of production, not only has Middle Eastern crude been restricted by import quotas, but it is now available at prices competitive with domestic sources that historically have been more expensive than imports by as much as $1 a barrel. Thus, the only way for small refiners and marketers to remain viable has been removed by the inflation in imported crude oil. Unbranded gas, used by both independents and majors to sell below standard retail prices, has all but disappeared from the retail markets. Gas prices within entire regions, if not throughout the country, are becoming more uniform, eliminating the space once occupied by the independent refiners and marketers.

II

From the marketers' perspective, the most distressing feature of the oil crisis is the absence of any new refining companies since 1950; and this is despite the enormous increase in the demand for oil at the retail level. The restrictions placed on the entrance of new refiners are intimately related to the unreliability of crude oil supplies and the control by the giant corporations over "free world" sources. Since the national government has been closely associated with the seven largest oil companies in the formulation of import quotas, energy and tax policy, it is not surprising to find that the government has acted to restrict the quantities of crude oil available for refining and, ultimately, for marketing.

These are not recent developments. For many years, the oil companies have complained that the economy was burdened with too much oil and that import quotas were necessary to protect domestic crude production, especially because foreign crude was produced under more efficient and, therefore, cheaper conditions. In view of the alleged glut of crude oil, oil companies claimed that there was no need to invest their capital in the expansion of refining capacity. In fact, in the mid-1960s many companies, especially in the Standard Oil group, were closing the older, less efficient plants without replacing them within the borders of the United States, building their new plants instead in Puerto Rico, the Virgin Islands, Aruba and even closer to sources of crude oil, in Venezuela and the Middle East. These plants were built not only to serve Latin America, the Caribbean area and Central America, but also the United States. A few large independents such as the Commonwealth Oil Refining Company, a Puerto Rican based corporation, and the Hess Corporation were responsible for some of the new facilities along with the big seven.

Much of the refined oil was used for petrochemical production as well as gasoline. Along with Texas and West Virginia, Puerto Rico became among the largest petrochemical centers within the United States orbit. Giants like Phillips, Gulf, Mobil and Shell were involved in the new refineries and in many cases, they built those facilities as joint projects just as the Aramco and the Anglo Iranian companies had formed combines in the Middle East.

In 1966, as a representative of the Oil, Chemical and Atomic Workers International Union, I became involved in both the shutting of the older plants and the development of the Caribbean Oil Refining centers. The oldest plant in the United States, the Mobil Refinery in Greenpoint, Brooklyn, was closed in 1966, except for a small compounding department. At the same time, the company shut its facility in Minnesota. The union could not prevent the company from closing the refineries, and had to content itself with winning substantial separation benefits for the workers. From the company's point of view, this way of settling the issues raised by closing the plants was a real bargain. Since the proportion of capital to living labor is extraordinarily high in the continuous flow technologies of the oil refinery industry, the problem of labor costs is relatively negligible. In the United States only 78,000 workers produce about 85 percent of the refined oil used in industry, homes and cars. But the amount of capital that must be invested, and the length of time required before the refinery is "on stream" (i.e., ready for operation) means that the shortages could have been produced by the failure to continue to invest in refining capacity within the United States in the face of increasing demand.

The steadily rising demand for refined oil both here and abroad has been no secret to either the industry or the government. The decision not to expand refining capacity in the face of increased consumption constituted nothing less than a strike by the major oil companies against the American people and the developing countries. The *reduced* production of refined oil in 1973 compared to 1972 reflected the refusal of the oil industry's giants to invest sufficient capital in new refining plants within the United States. Instead, refineries were built elsewhere; the corporations invested capital in coal and nuclear energy, and moved capital into the petrochemical industries.

There is another line of reasoning that must be taken into account if the full story is to be understood. In the early 1960s the oil companies claimed that their capacity was sufficient to meet present and future demands for refined petroleum, notwithstanding the shutdowns. Oil companies claimed that the problem was excess capacity, not the reverse. This argument was the basis of their restriction on expansion within the U.S., while the increasing demands for oil among the less developed countries of Latin America became the rationale for building in that area. From an economic perspective, construction of refineries close to the sources of crude oil supply were justifiable according to industry spokesmen. Yet by the last half of the decade, industry leaders were already warning that a crisis was brewing in the supplies of crude oil. The advent of the Vietnam war, the enormous increases in car production, the replacement of coal by oil and natural gas in heating homes were conspiring to force a reevaluation of the situation. The industry argued that unless the government moved to provide incentives to the industry to find new sources of crude oil and allow for the construction of new refineries, besides the available sources in Latin America, the Middle East and within the United States, the worldwide demand for oil would inevitably outrun supplies. The crisis could easily become apparent if Latin American or Middle Eastern oil-producing countries refused to increase their shipments to the United States in proportion to the depletion of internal sources, and if natural gas regulation was maintained so as to strangle the incentives to exploration.

In 1967, the president of Sun Oil Company and chairman of the American Petroleum Institute, Robert G. Dunlop, addressing the Institute's annual meeting, sounded the alarm on oil and natural gas exploration: "The one area of real concern," he said, "continues to be drilling for oil and gas. Results for the year to date indicate that both exploratory and development well completions will be off substantially in 1967. With demand continuing to advance steadily, this decline in drilling points to a potential supply problem in the future." [5]

Two years later H. Donald Borger, chairman and chief executive officer of the Consolidated Natural Gas Company, told the House Ways and Means Committee that "the reserve-production ratio [of natural gas] is approaching a level which most would describe as minimum." [6] Testifying before the Senate antimonopoly subcommittee Dunlop reported that the oil industry was "failing to find new supplies as fast as we were using existing reserves." [7] He cited ever rising demand for petroleum as the cause of depletion of oil reserves as well as government tax constraints that deflated incentives. Dunlop told the Senate Finance Committee that the "sharply rising oil-finding and development costs" were becoming prohibitive in terms of the possibility of stepping up exploration.

In 1971 Frank Ikard, Dunlop's successor as chairman of the API, reiterated these themes. Government regulatory and tax policies and the failure to provide incentives for exploration activities were creating conditions that would lead to grave shortages.

The oil industry had been stung by the reduction of the oil depletion allowance from 27 percent to 22 percent a few years earlier, in 1969. But the large corporations in oil and natural gas were not only concerned with federal regulatory policies or restrictions on tax write-offs; the pressure of citizen groups seeking to limit the sulphur content in fuels, their outcry against oil spills on the West Coast, their resistance to construction of new energy facilities—especially pipeline construction from the Alaska shelf—to nuclear plants near center cities, cracking plants with few safety protections, too were interpreted by the oil companies as a clear indication that the "atmosphere" within the United States was not conducive for investment. Predictions of rising consumer demand for energy thus did not constitute sufficient incentive for expansion of either refining facilities or of exploration and development activities.

So the most important feature of the crisis of 1973 was that it succeeded in altering government policy. Long-stalled projects such as the pipeline were quickly approved by Congress. Government price controls became an effective instrument for raising rather than stabilizing prices; and in view of the plentiful supply that was made available after prices rose by about 30 percent one suspects that the controls prevented a sharp reduction in prices that would have been possible in a genuinely free market. Actually, prices had been falling since the late 1950s. Oil company profits on the international barrel only began to fall in 1969. The government was enlisted by the oil and energy corporations to regulate the flow of crude oil from cheaper fields in the Middle East so as to keep the price of domestic and Latin American crude (both controlled by the oil giants) up. Not even the manifest shortages of heating and engine fuel at the retail level could persuade the government to relax significantly the oil import quotas. As we have pointed out, the quota—in addition to its price stabilization effect—had a decisive influence in preventing new refiners from entering the field during the 1950-1974 period. When it became evident that oil supplies were not significantly depleted, nor shipments from Arab countries reduced despite the "boycott," the game plan of the large energy corporations was more apparent.

Another critical feature of the crisis was the emergence of the new ideology of energy "self-sufficiency" enunciated by the Nixon administration. Ideology translated into policy in two fundamental areas. First, the revival of the coal industry as a substitute for oil, which was made possible by the vast reserves of this fossil fuel within the United States. All that was necessary to facilitate the growth of the coal industry was the relaxation of regulations governing the sulphur content in fuels, the ability of coal companies to undertake strip-mining in states that had enacted stringent environmental protections, and the cooperation of major manufacturing companies, utilities, and the general public in converting oil and natural gas burning furnaces to coal. Even though it looked as if the oil and natural gas corporations might suffer from the competition engendered by this policy, once it became known that oil companies had purchased many coal companies in the 1960s when prices for this seemingly moribund fuel were plummeting, there was no reason to shed tears for the oil giants. Their control of half of the major coal producers seems to have reduced worries over competition between coal and oil.

Now the remaining oil reserves, which conservation policies had kept intact, could be exploited. The American people would pay with higher fuel prices for the capital needed to explore underwater sources of oil within the United States, the Alaska shelf, and to steam shale from western rock. *The Wall Street Journal*, however, doubted that the self-sufficiency policy could be fulfilled, its major argument being that the high cost of such exploration and insufficient returns on investment would make it unlikely that self-sufficiency could be achieved without forcing the price of gasoline at the pump to $1 a gallon. The *Journal* failed to mention another factor preventing the fulfillment of Nixon's dream of a balanced economy.

United States investments in Middle Eastern and other sources of crude oil have contributed heavily to the chronic U.S. balance of payments deficit. Since oil investments account for almost one half of all U.S. foreign investments, it represents an important factor for the entire U.S. economy. For many years, oil profits in the Middle East have been largely exempt from domestic taxation. Since, until now, only a very small proportion of these profits has been reinvested in the Middle Eastern countries (the greater part always having reverted to the United States-based operations) the annual balance of payments deficit due to overseas oil investments amounted to about $750 million in 1969. This means that a policy of self-sufficiency is not in the interest of U.S. capital. Sufficient reserves exist elsewhere, and are currently being exploited with the assistance of United States investments, to meet world energy requirements until 1985. The oil companies with important Middle Eastern and Latin American holdings are caught in a quandary. On the one hand, the size of their overseas investments and the high profits accruing from them make it improbable that they will surrender control in these areas. In this connection, the concession to Saudi Arabia granted in 1974 by the oil companies whereby the rich Middle Eastern oil nation took over 60% "ownership" does not signal the end of foreign domination of the area's oil reserves. Even though the OPEC (oil producing and exporting countries) are likely to continue to exact more of the profits, they will still rely on the big combines for processing, distribution and marketing as well as the management of the fields and the construction of new refineries.

On the other hand, there has been a substantial acceleration of domestic exploration activities since the crisis became acute in 1973. Offshore drilling on both the Atlantic and Pacific coasts has stepped up considerably. Government auction of oil-rich shale lands has brought high prices. The next step, undoubtedly, will be a major effort by the large oil corporations to restore the depletion allowance to its old level. And this will create the conditions for a substantial rise in the wholesale and retail prices of fuel so that capital can be raised for exploration activities, refinery construction, and corporate-sponsored development activities in the third world.

Thus, the evidence points in two directions: The oil companies are holding on tenaciously in the Middle East and Latin America and, at the same time, working furi-

ously to implement the "self sufficiency" energy policy as
a guarantee against future losses.

The concept of national self-sufficiency also serves a
rationale for allowing oil prices to rise and for promoting coal as a major fuel source. As for natural gas, regulations that tended to depress the price of this important
fuel, if lifted, could result in the exploration of important
new reserves, for example, off the Long Island coast.
Here, of course, the ecological issue will once again be
raised because residents of the area have consistently resisted efforts by natural gas companies to gain access to
these reserves.

"Arab nationalism" was conveniently exploited by the
oil companies and the leading producer nations to force
up the price of crude by nearly 500 percent. There was
no likelihood of expropriation of the Aramco or Anglo
Iranian properties. Arab nations did exact concessions
from United States companies. They were promised
higher royalty payments, U.S. and corporate aid in development activities within some of the oil-producing
countries, and other smaller benefits. But they did not
demand that the oil monopolies relinquish control, even
though on the surface the oil companies appeared to agree
to a stepped-up timetable for increasing OPEC nations'
share of ownership.

The self-sufficiency call may affect two other important
aspects of energy development in this country. First, the
long-disputed development of nuclear energy may be enhanced by the threat of future shortages. Chemical companies, together with electrical and power corporations
have been pressing for new concessions from the Atomic
Energy Commission and from local communities for nuclear plant construction for at least fifteen years. The traditional objections of the communities that large-scale nuclear energy manufacturing is too dangerous have success-

fully prevented nuclear power from displacing oil and coal as major energy sources until now. In the past, oil companies were known to be instrumental in fighting the introduction of nuclear energy, as were the coal companies which figured to suffer most directly from the use of nuclear fuel in the production of electric power.

But oil companies have had, and will continue to have, an enormous volume of surplus profits to invest. Instead of using their capital to expand domestic refining capacity, search for alternate sources such as geothermal, fusion or solar energy, the oil companies have invested capital in the manufacture of oil-based chemicals such as plastics, synthetic rubber, and other inorganic industrial materials and have even begun to invest in entirely unrelated fields. Recently the Mobil Oil Company purchased Marco, the holding company of Montgomery Ward, a leading chain retailer. They have diversified to coal and have shown an interest in entering into joint ventures in the construction of nuclear plants.

There is evidence that the time for nuclear energy may be at hand, and higher oil prices may be a vehicle for expanding the entrance of the oil companies into this field. On March 23, 1974, *Business Week* ran a story reporting the entrance of new "competition in Atomic Power": the General Atomic Company, a corporation jointly owned by Royal Dutch/Shell and the Gulf Corporation. Their first project, the construction of a plant for Public Service Company of Colorado, will utilize new technologies and the considerable quantities of capital available to the company to enter the nuclear power industry. G.A. hopes to develop a way to produce nuclear power that will prove safer than the current methods that have excited considerable opposition. If they can convince the Atomic Energy Commission and many local communities of the superiority of their methods, the oil companies may become important nuclear energy producers, and the competition among a variety of energy alternatives will become a specter of the past.

III

We are witnessing the most massive concentration of economic power in the history of the world. The part played by energy in the industrial process is so crucial that the takeover by oil giants of the primary, the refining and the marketing sectors of the petroleum industry, their growing domination of the coal industry, their entrance as a prime producer into nuclear and other new sources of energy means that the seven major corporations are making a bid for decisive control over the world's energy resources. The "energy crisis" was engineered to provide the political conditions for achieving this major objective of the oil companies. By entirely capturing marketing, refining and crude supplies, the oil companies have made sure that the Middle Eastern countries would have few "outs" in the face of a unified industry here in the United States, even if they successfully expropriated the large corporations.

The rise in the world price of crude oil has already had a profound effect on the development strategies of a number of Asian, African and Latin American nations. These countries, having barely begun to construct the preconditions for industrialization, have been set back by the rising costs of energy. India has been particularly hard hit by the rise of Middle Eastern crude prices. Its own balance of payments deficit has been substantially increased, as has the international position of many other countries which are dependent on external sources of oil. It may be that the thwarting of development within the third world was an unintended consequence of the petroleum crisis, but it cannot help but strengthen the position of the metropolitan countries in the third world areas. Among the new possibilities is that oil companies will be invited to explore and exploit energy resources in India, Pakistan and other oil-poor countries. But, being forced to take this road cannot help but raise the whole cold war specter once more for the developing nations. Their already fragile policy of "nonalignment" is bound to disintegrate if crucial concessions are made to large oil monopolies. Thus the Middle Eastern moves to raise crude oil prices will have a crucial effect on the unified third world posture against intervention by both the United States and the Soviet Union. Economic self-interest is forcing an alliance between the Middle Eastern and other oil producing countries and the supranational oil corporations rather than an African-Asian Latin American alliance. The development strategies of oil producers have substantially shifted toward an accommodation with the oil corporations as the best assurance of economic growth.

The concern that Middle Eastern states will deal separately with European and Japanese buyers of oil, thereby undercutting the dominant role of the United States, cannot be taken too seriously. This theory is based on the assumption that United States oil majors are not intimately involved in the production and distribution of Middle Eastern oil, a theory simply not supported by the evidence. The two giant oil producing combines, controlled in the main by Rockefeller, BP and Royal Dutch/Shell interests, retain their power in the Middle East and Latin America, the two major sources of crude oil in the capitalist world.

The dependence of Europe and Japan on foreign oil supplies is bound to accelerate their woes, particularly because of the higher prices being asked by producing countries. These higher prices will place strains on the currency position of these countries, raise new problems for their own exports, and indirectly enhance the strength of the dollar. Flowing from this set of relationships is the likelihood that the oil crisis served indirectly to assist the United States to pull out of its interrelated balance of payments and monetary crisis. By forcing European competitors to pay more for food and fuel, the price advantages of European and Japanese exporters were effectively wiped out. The dollar successfully recovered in European money markets and the overseas investments of the U.S.-based supranationals were safeguarded. Europe and Japan found themselves once more in a dependent position. The dream of the Common Market as a third great superpower seemed temporarily stalled by the aftermath of the inflation in the price of raw materials. This development may serve to erase the last vestiges of Western European and Japanese autonomy from the supranational United States based giants.

In short, the oil crisis signals the emergence of monopolization of the Western capitalist world and Japan in fewer hands than ever before. The oil companies have made their move, and appear to have been successful. The reverberations within the United States are as powerful as those in other countries. An immediate consequence is the changing shape of the all-important car industry. Ford and Chrysler are already making plans to convert almost entirely to compact cars that feature higher gas mileage. The auto makers were caught napping during the oil crisis and moved rapidly to recover ground lost by their failure to anticipate it. They had planned to place their emphasis on large and medium-sized cars in 1973 rather than on smaller models. The minuscule American Motors Corporation, on the other hand, showed its ability to increase its share of the auto market by making compact cars.

As thousands of workers were laid off by the big three to make possible the conversion of assembly lines to smaller cars (70,000 workers were permanently furloughed), the General Motors Corporation hesitated to follow its competitors into the smaller-car field. Instead of large-scale conversion it only expanded its smaller-car line slightly, insisting that so-called intermediate cars and big models would still find substantial numbers of buyers. Either the GM managers were willing to bank on the end of the energy crunch, at least the end of the long lines at the gas pumps, or they were anticipating a reduction in gas prices that would encourage a resurgence of sales of the larger models, or they were satisfied to reduce GM's share of the car market. That share had been reduced from more than 45 percent of all United States domestic sales to about 37 percent in the first quarter of 1974. The question raised in the industry was whether GM knew something that had escaped the other auto producers.

Amid widespread predictions that gas prices would not only remain high but would increase at a rate of about 4 percent a year, even if the oil shortage should abate, the slow rate of changeover by GM's management appeared suicidal. The only possible explanation short of sheer incompetence is that GM was planning to move more heavily into producing other goods. The two possibilities were that GM would join General Electric as the major producer of new mass transit equipment that would be needed to overcome the effects of energy shortages and inflationary trends, and secondly, that the company was anticipating an increase in military production that might justify its relatively sanguine approach to the decline in auto sales.

By 1974 both possibilities appeared likely. Mass transit construction was a clear alternative to high rates of auto construction, especially if the big corporations could find some benefit in it. Secondly, the 1974 rate of military spending was eight billion dollars higher than the previous year when the Vietnam war was still providing the key justification for large chunks of the military budget. Since GM is a major defense contractor, it appeared reasonable that its chagrin about the decline of auto sales, produced in part by the so-called energy crisis, could be successfully suppressed.

Yet the possibility remained that GM was not simply sitting still watching its production and sales of cars decrease, but was preparing for a decrease in oil prices and a resumption of business as usual. This possibility was suggested by the theory that inflated prices of both crude and refined oil were expedients employed by the largest oil companies to tighten their grip on all sectors of the industry, but that prices would be reduced once the medium-sized refiners and marketing chains were driven out of business or reduced in size and influence.

In any case, the changes in car industry was just one example of the sudden transformations engendered by the energy crisis. In other areas, small- and medium-sized chemical and plastics manufacturers using oil-based raw materials were discovering that the prices for these products had become prohibitive. Thousands of workers were laid off by employers whose share of the government-controlled oil allocations was substantially reduced during the crisis. The larger petrochemical producers, often owned by the larger oil companies, were supplied with greater quantities of feedstock and not substantially hurt by the energy shortages. They were able to gain new markets at the expense of the energy-starved smaller companies.

The entrance of the oil companies into the chemical industry was not a new development. Their drive toward absolute power within the petrochemical branches was facilitated by the crisis. Thus, as the worst effects of the oil shortages were said to be at an end with the lifting of the Arab oil embargo in March, 1974, the shape of American industry was substantially altered from a year earlier. Small producers of all kinds of oil, coal and natural gas-based products were freely predicting the end to competition not only in the primary sectors of these industries, but in the secondary branches as well. Vertical integration by the supranational energy corporations was given a huge boost by the crisis. In this connection, it would be a gross error to assume that the major leaps in profits for the last quarter of 1973 and the first quarter of the following year were the result of greed alone.

The crisis helped raise capital for the acquisition of smaller companies, helped facilitate conglomerate developments in other energy fields, and helped restore the position of the oil companies that deteriorated during the period of price stability between the late 1950s to the early 1970s.

# 4

# Consequences of the Crisis

---

The food and energy crises are symptoms of an enormous shift underway in the configuration of American economic, political and social life. We are witnessing a strategic reversal of the fortunes of the United States economy. As compared to the dominant trend of the post-World War II period toward alternate spurts of war-induced economic growth and stagnation, the internal economy is entering a long-term period of decline. Industrial production within the United States itself will continue to stagnate, or may even show a significant downturn. The public sector, whose expansion was a characteristic feature of the past two decades, has already begun to contract. The end of expansion of education, health and other publicly supported services is a reflection of the fact that they are financed by taxes on wages and salaries which, in turn, have suffered owing to the rising inflationary trend, increased unemployment and the consequent downturn in real wages.

In short, the United States is losing its privileged position in the world economy. The working class, which has enjoyed a higher level of real wages than any advanced capitalist country, is being asked to accept an international equalization of wages and living standards. The higher prices for food and fuel are a symptom of this trend. Like their European counterparts, the American working class, and substantial sections of the middle class, are now forced to spend a higher portion of their income on such absolute essentials as food, clothing and fuel than any time since World War II. The significant portion of income available for durables—housing, cars, appliances, furniture and "leisure" hardware such as boats and camping equipment—has shrunk considerably.

We have recently discovered the sustained importance of agricultural and industrial raw materials for maintaining the international trade position of the United States-based multinationals. Both food and energy are crucial commodities in the unending struggle to buttress the value of the American dollar in the face of expanding international commitments. In the past thirty-five years, three wars and an enormous expansion of overseas investment produced chronic instability in this country's international trade position. Although the worldwide character of United States capital served to catalyze inflationary trends at home, in contrast, it enhanced United States power abroad.

The late 1950s and 1960s were marked by the simultaneous emergence of Europe and Japan as viable economies, and the relative decline of the preeminence of United States manufactured products. Only the amazing

productivity of United States agriculture and the tremendous refining capacity of United States oil industries
that allowed oil exports and high rates of domestic consumption at the same time, prevented a major depression
after the Vietnam war. United States capital is not out of
the woods. It must mobilize an ever-increasing proportion
of American agricultural resources and consolidate its
control over resources for the domestic and international
economy in order to safeguard its world position.

The short-term cause of the steep inflation in food and
energy prices and products that depend on these basic
commodities was the attempt by the government to solve
the balance of payments crisis and safeguard capital values
abroad. A slower, less perceptible reason why retail and
wholesale prices keep rising is this: Contrary to the popular assumption that food was among our last competitive
industries, food growing, processing, and marketing have
fallen increasingly under the monopolistic control of a
few banks, conglomerates and holding corporations.
Aided by the Federal Government, these corporations
have been permitted to regulate food supplies for domestic consumption as well as encouraged to divert substantial
quantities of crops for foreign trade. They have been permitted to rationalize food processing in a way injurious
not only to the consumer's pocketbook, but also to the
public's health. Similarly, distribution and marketing are
now under the control of a relatively few chain stores that
have effectively eliminated the independent grocer, and
are, in turn, controlled by the same corporations that have
assumed power over growing and processing. The vertical integration of the food industry was the inevitable result of the entrance of large capital into this sector. These
large corporations regard the food industry as just another
source of investment that is expected to yield the same

rates of profit possible in any other manufacturing or service industry. This development has reversed the long-term role that agriculture has played in the American economy as a source of capital accumulation by providing cheap food and allowing lower wage levels than would otherwise have been possible. In the same manner, the grab by the oil companies of many of the largest coal producers not only signals the revival of this once moribund industry, but means that the United States can no longer rely on cheap energy as an underpinning of its economic growth. As I have shown, not only have the petroleum sectors been integrated under the control of seven giant and mutually cooperative oil companies, but all the major energy resources of the capitalist world have been subsumed by these supranationals.

The most immediate effects of the successful bid by the oil corporations to control energy have been felt by the would-be competitors of Europe and Japan. The energy crisis signals nothing less than the return of the world economic power relationships to the status quo of 1950 with one essential difference: the separation of nations from each other is now more problematic than ever before. Interdependence is no longer the wildest dream of a liberal corporate reformer like Wendell Willkie, who proclaimed the era of one world in cornucopian terms thirty years ago. It is now a reality, but there is no utopia attached to it.

"One World" means the nearly complete control of the world economy by a relatively few United States-based multinational corporations and their junior partners in Europe and Japan. The idea of competition is applicable to the world economy in one sense only: the persistent conflict between international and national corporations in all advanced capitalistic countries. But the terms of the competition are by no means equal.

The national capitalist classes of Western countries and the United States have suffered a progressive deterioration in both their political and their economic positions since the First World War. What is new about the present situation is that their voices have been virtually silenced. In the United States, neither the arch conservatives nor the welfare statists were able to mount anything like an effective protest against the manipulation that came to the surface during the twin crises. They were disorganized, and, for the most part, disoriented. To be sure, congressional hearings continued to bring to the surface information that showed incontrovertibly the lying, the profit-grabbing and the strategic aims of the larger corporations. Many public officials are "shocked and saddened," but they have been reduced to hand-wringing. Some reformers, particularly those associated with the enviromental movement, actually welcomed the possibility of shortages. This myopic vision only helped to strengthen the claims of the oil and food monopolies that austerity was good for the moral fiber of the country.

The only coherent opposition to the relentless drive of the oil and food groups was provided by the impotent but numerically important middle class, white-collar and professional groups. Unfortunately consumers and independent truck owner-operators lack the social power and the vision to give lasting voice to the opposition. Their activities proved sporadic, even if colorful. The most important accomplishment of these movements against rising food prices and manipulated energy shortages has been educational. But they are engaged in an essentially rearguard action, because they are still oriented toward the pluralistic model of government and are really powerless to reverse the tide of monopoly power.

The most vocal demands of consumer movements have been directed at altering government policy. But the trouble with this thrust is that the government itself both initiates and responds to the national and international needs of the supranational corporations. It is the instrument of a definite interest in the conflict. The record since the First World War shows that the government's intervention into agricultural and energy matters has been consistent regardless of the political party in power. It has been mobilized to regulate and coordinate the interests of the largest corporations in their external and internal business relations.

Government policies have been directed toward restricting production and maintaining high levels of corporate profits in these industries because of the relatively restricted market situation. Second, the Federal Government has acted swiftly to protect the value of United States capital investments in overseas markets by mobilizing farm products as a key export commodity. Third, the government has regulated credit and other fiscal relationships to allow the greatest amount of buying of goods at home and abroad. Finally, the Federal Government has assisted the perpetuation of the permanent war economy buttressed by a permanent war psychosis in order to close the chronic gap between production and consumption that arose in the 1920s and 1930s.

I

Among the most important long-range effects of the recent crises is that the tremendous increases of profits accruing to the oil companies are likely to change the development strategies of Third World countries and the investment strategies of the oil monopolies. For nearly a hundred years, Asia, Africa and Latin America have been valuable to Western capitalism primarily as sources of raw materials and as sources of a cheap reserve labor supply to be employed with the advanced countries during periods of capital expansion. Raw materials development has accounted for more than half of United States capital investments abroad. European capital too has found its way into underdeveloped countries for the purpose of raw materials extraction. In the coming years, this type of investment will occupy a diminished place among advanced capitalist countries. Instead, the trend, already evident in Europe after the Second World War, for United States capital and administration to find outlets in the development of manufacturing industries and even service industries will likely be extended to the developing countries.

From the point of view of the supranationals, the extension of their investment plans to include manufactured products reflects the diminished outlets for capital investment in the most developed part of the world. Recent evidence of stagnation within western European countries indicates that the steep ascent of their economies has come to an end. As in the United States, other countries—France, Britain, West Germany and other major European industrial nations—are suffering from runaway inflation, reflecting the disproportion between the productive sector and the proliferation of the nonproductive service sector. In addition, these countries are beginning to experience deficits in their trade balances in part due to the devaluation of the U.S. dollar and the skyrocketing prices of imports of food and oil.

Second, the large international corporations are setting their investment targets on developing countries because of the fear of expropriation if some concessions are not made. The demands of the developing countries themselves for loans and gifts to help overcome their dependence on the advanced countries fit neatly into the need for new outlets for capital. The oil monopolies that dominate Middle East crude production are no longer in a position to deny the aspirations of the restless Arabian national capitalist class. The recent diplomatic and economic struggle resulted in a partial victory for the Arabs within a restricted framework. They won concessions in terms of promises of capital investment and technical assistance for their almost nonexistent manufacturing sector, in return for which they agreed to the long-term presence of the two major oil monopolies in the area. A parallel trend was evident in Latin America, particularly Venezuela, which is the richest oil-producing country on that continent. It may be that the Nixon doctrine of "self-sufficiency" can vitiate the extent of concessions. But it seems clear that the oil companies themselves are determined to invest capital in new sectors.

In the light of the considerable accumulated wealth possessed by the supranationals and the limited opportunities available within the United States, this new development strategy is eminently reasonable. It is not being forged without turbulence, however. One of the preconditions for increasing the size of investment in manufacturing and service industries overseas is the preparation of the American people for a lower standard of living. American workers are destined to compete in a number of industries with their foreign counterparts. In order to maintain the stability of crucial balance of payments, wages within the U.S. in labor-intensive industries must be held down. The wage factor in highly capital-intensive industries is relatively unimportant in the manufacturing process, but differential construction and transportation costs do depend, to a large extent, on wage levels. Competition in low wage industries has existed since the late 1950s. The new feature of the world economic situation is the internationalization of capital-intensive industries.

The establishment of a single international economy is

not a short-term task. Nor will underdevelopment be eliminated in third world countries or in the United States. A
certain amount of unevenness in the world economy is
helpful for insuring that plentiful supplies of cheap, mo-
bile labor are available for growth. Secondly, the political
and economic dependence of the Third World (translated
as a favorable climate for investment) is in the interest of
corporations within the advanced world. The creation of
oil refineries, petrochemical complexes and service industries within oil-producing countries is now entirely probable. Already such plants have been constructed in Puerto
Rico, other parts of the Caribbean, and the Middle East.
There is no reason to believe that this strategy will not be
extended elsewhere.

Beyond outlets for investment for primary oil producers, new areas of development provide a way to cut the
national capitalist class in on the action. For example, the
long-starved machine-tool industries and companies that
produce farm equipment within the United States are
bound to welcome any programs that result in the expansion of orders.* From the perspective of the supranationals
such orders serve to suppress possible opposition generated by the inflationary spiral among its own nationally
oriented corporate class. Among the corporations likely to
take advantage of the opportunities for investment in developing nations, the auto and electrical industry rank
high. The pace of construction of overseas parts and assembly plants by the General Motors and Chrysler corporations has accelerated over the past few years. Indeed,
these two giants were as self-interested as the oil companies in solving the balance of trade and monetary
crises in order to safeguard the value of their heavy capi-

---

* Sales to the Soviet Union in the 1970s assisted the machine-tool industry to recover from its longterm slump.

tal outlays abroad.° Similarly, electrical corporations, IBM and the rubber corporations have a deep stake in the direction of United States foreign trade and investment. The failure of these formidable economic powers to protest loudly against rising food prices and the oil price spiral is a sign that their own interests have shifted considerably to other markets. It is entirely probable that they are prepared to withstand a substantial reduction in domestic consumption of durable goods such as cars, electrical appliances and new housing as long as they are able to create new markets elsewhere for their substantial capital surpluses.

A final aspect of the international situation should be mentioned. Although the Soviet Union supplies much of its own energy needs because it is among the world's leading producers of coal and oil, it is interested in both Middle East oil and American food. The détente between the United States and the Soviet Union is rooted to a large extent in the chronic agricultural crisis within the latter and the immense productivity of the former. The United States needs the Soviet Union for two purposes: first, to bail it out by expanding trade when necessary against the weakening dollar and second, possibly to help mediate relations between the oil companies and the Arabs.

As for mainland China, having failed to establish an independent southeast Asian economic bloc, it will probably move closer toward accommodation with the United States even though it is attempting to negotiate from a position of strength. The iron grip that United States-based corporations have established over much of the world's supply of energy places China in an analogous

---

° General Motors has actually entered the energy business. It is interested in nuclear developments and may join oil companies in financing the exploration of other energy sources. This helps explain GM's silence during the spurt of fuel prices in late 1973 and the spring of 1974.

structural position with any other developing country. If substantial quantities of crude oil could be found within its borders, China would undoubtedly seek European, Japanese and United States sources of capital for the purposes of development. This is not an ideological retreat. It must be faced as the price any nation will have to pay for industrialization in the future. Its main alternatives to this concession, a closer tie to the Soviet Union or another "great leap forward" in its capacity to generate capital by its own bootstraps, cannot be overlooked as concomitant strategies. The Chinese have appeared at the world energy conferences with a rhetorically more militant and anti-imperialist stance than at any time since the middle of the Vietnam war. Chinese militance is undoubtedly connected to its attempt to make alliances with other nations seriously set back by the rising oil prices—principally India, Pakistan and Japan.

China's efforts to take a leading role in the creation of a developing nations' bloc against the United States and the Soviet Union are likely to become an important element in its diplomatic policy. However, the terms of the bargain are not likely to change the international relationship of economic and political forces, at least in the short run. Despite the great advances in such programs of economic self-sufficiency such as the diversification of rural communes to include manufacturing as well as agricultural production, China will require heavy capital inputs to explore its own mineral resources such as metals for nuclear production, oil and coal. It may also cooperate with American investors to develop its considerable water resources.

II

Among the most remarkable features of the recent crisis was the relative ease with which energy producers and agribusinesses were able to impose their will on the American nation. One explanation has already been given: contrary to the early views of such economists as John Kenneth Galbraith, the countervailing forces within business have all but disappeared.

The same cannot be said for the entire society. But, neither the pluralistic model of American politics nor the competitive model of American business has been operative for more than a half-century. Yet there was a dramatic semblance of competition dramatically shown within the higher circles of American corporate relationships in the 1960s. Analyzing the shape of American politics and economic life in that period, some writers saw a mortal struggle between Yankees and Cowboys. The fight for control over government and business was raging between the representatives of old "Wall Street" capital, particularly the Rockefeller and the Morgan interests, and the emerging challengers from the west and southwest, such institutions as the Bank of America controlling a large share of agricultural business, the aircraft corporations, the contending medium-sized oil companies (but large by conventional business standards) and finally, the glamorous, fast-moving new conglomerates based on money juggling. The image of David and Goliath was invoked more than once to describe this conflict. The singular figure who epitomized the new "money managers" was James Ling whose company, Ling-Temco-Vought, actually succeeded in wresting control from the easterners over the fourth-largest steel producer—Jones and Laughlin. Within a few years, Ling had been crushed and the managerial palace revolution seemed to have been suppressed.

Yet, during the Vietnam war period there was some basis for believing that a conflict was raging within the higher circles of American capitalism. Battles over control within large corporations were only one feature of the conflict. To the extent that the government is closely entwined with big business, the struggle for power extended to the political arena. Prior to the 1968 party conventions, Nelson Rockefeller came forward as a serious contender for the Republican Presidential nomination. From the start his bid seemed ill-fated because the machinery of the Republican Party had been successfully taken over by the most conservative elements. Their power was made absolutely evident in the Goldwater coup of 1964, but, despite a humiliating defeat at the polls, the professional politicians who rose to power during the Goldwater campaign were able to keep the reins of the party.

Richard Nixon's nomination by the Republicans in 1968 was assured by the iron grip of the conservatives over the party machinery and the huge sums advanced by the "cowboy" (Western) group of American corporations. In turn, Nixon came to power with the support of the military —a distinct political interest in this country that has recently allied itself with those corporations most intimately involved in the production of military hardware and services.

The episode of the intracorporate struggle for power seems ended, at least on its recent terms. Although Nixon was able to forestall an early end to the Vietnam war against the expressed wishes of Eastern financial groups whose economic interests were being hurt by both the large volume of overseas expenditures due to the war and the inflationary impact of high levels of domestic military spending, he was unable to maintain his political autonomy after the defeat of the Cowboys. After 1971, he ran Wall Street's errands, including the establishing of closer ties with Mainland China, cementing the détentist trend of United States-Soviet relations and effecting a major shift in the emphasis of United States foreign policy to the problems of international competition with European and Japanese capital.

In retrospect, the Yankee-Cowboy struggle seems little more than a skirmish. The reigns of corporate power are held to an amazing extent by the old corporate groups centered around eastern financial corporations. The attempt to construct a force powerful enough to challenge traditional banking and industrial interests, could only be based on the maintenance of the war economy as the most significant feature of economic expansion and capital accumulation. The period of the entrance of the challengers into the higher circles of corporate decision-making coincided with the rise of the defense industries during the Vietnam war, the expansion of the service sectors, the appearance of national conglomeration as a significant feature of the American economy and the easing of credit in order to facilitate the expansion of all types of consumption and investment.

The decision by the largest corporations to end the United States involvement in the war was intimately bound to the deterioration of the dollar's position abroad. But it may have also been prompted by the requirements of the intercorporate struggle, to the extent that the new capitalists posed a threat to the hegemony of the Morgans, Rockefellers, Du Ponts, Mellons and Eatons, among others. The struggle against the space program, the raising of interest rates, the energy crisis itself, were all measures that were directed toward ending the material basis of the power of the nationally oriented Cowboy capitalists. In the main, the strategy of induced recession to achieve this goal was eminently successful.

The balance of payments and monetary crises were handled in perfect harmony with the interests of the financial and industrial groupings who are largely international in scope. The so-called "national capitalists," that is, those who conduct most or all of their operations in the specifically United States market, were almost totally eclipsed. Nixon's friends among the independent or medium-sized oil and other energy corporations suffered enormous defeats during the crisis, as did those smaller producers in the steel, chemical and consumer goods industries as a whole. The transformation of farm interests into satellites of the international business groups was virtually complete.

The independent capitalists who supported a right-wing alternative to the dominant pattern of United States multinationalism, which determines United States foreign policy, have largely lost their social power. Moreover, there is no basis for believing that a liberal-led coalition can provide an articulate program to establish government policies that depart radically from the consensus and still remain within a corporate capitalist framework. The options for locating sources of effective opposition to the supranationals have narrowed.

In 1911, the German socialist Rudolf Hilferding advanced an interpretation of the internationalization of capital in terms that suggested the possibility that imperialist nations could cooperate sufficiently to create a kind of superimperialism directed by finance capital. The organization of the entire world by a few capitalist nations would forestall a world imperialist war and create the material conditions for the transition to a socialist (*i.e.*, a centralized) economy. Organized capitalism, according to Hilferding, would achieve the full integration of the national capitalist states with the international capitalist economy.

Lenin's harsh judgment on this view was certainly borne out by the outbreak of World War I, which he found to be nothing but the reflection of divisions among imperialist powers, the proof of the importance of national capitals contending in the international marketplace for economic and political hegemony. Lenin discovered in the law of uneven development a theoretical explanation for the existence of international competition. When Germany, the United States and Japan entered their capitalist maturity, they could no longer find outlets for investment within their own national markets. The export of capital, however, created the objective basis for conflict with those capitalists who had already divided the world into spheres of influence (read: territories for capital investment based on the extraction of raw materials). The military and political conflict was the inevitable result of the late entrance of these upstart imperialists who were now demanding a redivision of the world.

According to Lenin, the second aspect of unevenness, the relatively underdeveloped nature of the colonial and semicolonial world, constituted the principal catalyst for world revolution. In Lenin's view, the imperialists of the metropolitan countries deliberately held the colonial and semicolonial world in bondage. This dependence was achieved by a careful pattern of capital investment that concentrated within the extractive industries and the infrastructure such as transport and communications networks needed for shipping raw materials to the market. At the same time, the exploited, underdeveloped countries were not allowed to employ their own resources for the purposes of accumulating capital and, in turn, reinvesting in manufacturing, scientific and service industries. Thus the colonial countries would remain impoverished because they would be required to import all types of manufactured goods. Even where the colonial country possessed rich farmland as in Brazil, Cuba and areas in Africa, the dependent nation would be forced to depend on a single crop, say, sugar or coffee and find markets only in the metropolitan country from which capital flowed.

The elements of a national bourgeoisie were called into being by imperialism, however. These were the traders, the struggling merchants, independent manufacturers, service professionals. In Lenin's view, the nascent middle class of these countries were revolutionary because the ideology of nationalism meant the expropriation of the imperialists. However, this class was not powerful enough to expel the imperialists unless it forged an alliance with the revolutionary workers and peasants. Thus, the revolution would break out in the weakest link of the imperialist chain, the "client" countries who resented the fact that their economies were undeveloped, imbalanced and restricted to relations with their own imperialist powers.

This is not the place to discuss the history of world imperialism since World War I in order to evaluate Lenin's theory. One observation may be offered however. The revolutions of national independence occurred much as Lenin predicted. In most cases, the national capitalists were too weak to carry the revolution to the end. In most instances, the failure to transform the national independence movement into a socialist revolution, as Lenin predicted, is a general phenomenon of the post-World War II situation. The advanced capitalist powers have successfully reappropriated most of the former colonial world, the main difference being that national political independence has been achieved. Yet these new nations are largely still under the control or substantial influence of the major imperialist powers. The national bourgeoisie, has become a *comprador bourgeoisie*, that is, an ally of the major international corporations. Even where governments within the former colonies wish for socialism or alternative forms of economic life, the economic dependency prevents the development of more than a rhetorical independence.

The power of the United States, France and Britain to contain the economic and social transformation of the Third World, even as it absorbed the revolutionary upsurge within its own tolerance for *political* self-determination, is a remarkable and pervasive feature of the past thirty years. Even the affiliation of some revolutions to the Chinese or Soviet blocs has failed to provide more than a small measure of economic independence. The best the developing nations have been able to achieve is to use the historic competition between the United States and the Soviet Union, more in evidence just after World War II than in the 1960s and 1970s, to obtain a measure of basic industrial development. Thus India and Egypt spearheaded the ideology of nonalignment as the best chance for overcoming the chronic economic dependence of the Arab and Asian countries. Cuba and China chose a closer tie with the Soviet Union. But this proved to be no solution for the objective of developing a balanced and independent economy, although it was useful for preventing these countries from being reabsorbed within the United States orbit. The new stage of imperialism that we are entering may constitute a vindication of Hilferding's premature thesis of organized world capitalism. Since World War II the world has teetered on the brink of such a development. The economic revival of western Europe and Japan in the 1950s and 1960s seemed to substantiate the assumption of continued international conflict between capitalist powers. It was upon this basis that the Soviet Union fashioned its own policy of peaceful coexistence with capitalist states, hoping to operate within the cleavages among capitalist countries in order to promote its program of trade with the West, shares in the development of natural resources in the "East," and security for its own post-World War II gains, particularly the acceptance of the eastern European area as a Soviet protectorate.

The specter of organized capitalism has been raised by the energy crisis at home and abroad. It may be no more than a paradigm of the "new society" as envisaged by U.S.-based multinationals. But in the past five years the vision of Luce's American Century has been more secure than at any time since the end of the Second World War. This new alliance will have to include Europe and Japan as important but subordinate, partners. Even sections of the domestic corporations must be cut in. Still, the dominant voices of the supranationals are now being heard around the world. As I have already noted, organized international capitalism emerges in contradiction to the historic autonomy of European, Japanese and United States nation states. As Sol Yurick has argued,* the modern world is witnessing the appearance of a kind of "metanation" of multinational corporations who constitute a second world government—making its own rules, recruiting and training its own police forces and army, and capturing governments and subordinating them to its will. Among the crucial examples of the takeover was the collapse of the Gaullist effort to constitute a new center for a second major capitalist power in the world.

De Gaulle's dream of a unified Europe able to deal equally with the United States and the Soviet Union on the basis of a high degree of economic self-sufficiency has been shattered. The elements of national capital that remain in Europe are disappearing as rapidly as in the United States. Multinationalism does not denote a complete colonization of Europe by the United States. In-

---

* I am indebted to Mr. Yurick for letting me see an unpublished manuscript in which this concept is developed.

stead, it describes the mobilization of sections of European capital by the U.S.-based corporations and the free movement of managerial personnel as well as capital between national borders. Among the most interesting examples of this tendency is the appointment of a Frenchman to be managing director of IBM International. Similarly, American corporations abroad are often managed by European nationals and though boards of directors of the new international corporations are dominated by the United States members, they include Europeans and Japanese.

III

The economic hegemony of the supranational corporations in the capitalist world has been forged under peculiar circumstances. The paradox of the new world economic situation is that the *national* economy of the United States has been considerably weakened since the end of the Vietnam war even as the U.S.-based international corporations have been strengthening their hold over the world economic system. First, the home economy suffers from sluggish production. The economy as a whole has shown almost no real growth since 1971, even though some sectors continue to expand. The slowing of production is revealed by the continuing trend toward the expansion of nongoods-producing labor such as clerical workers, service workers and administrative personnel generally. The transformation of the role of the United States from the overwhelmingly most-important-goods-producing nation into the world's financial and administrative center reflects the emergence of the multinational corporations and their ability to divert a considerable portion of capital investment to the goods-producing sectors of other countries.

Of course, the trend is by no means uniform in relation to all industries. Investments within the United States in capital goods, that is, the production of raw materials and machinery, remain relatively high compared to new advances in consumer goods, which are being made elsewhere. To a certain extent, the disparity between investments in the two sectors is designed to foster the dependent position of other nations on the United States. The program of constructing assembly plants of all kinds in Spain, Turkey and other developing countries, or transferring the centers of shoe, electronics and garment production to other areas indicates that the pattern of U.S. investment abroad will remain geared to perpetuating the imbalances within the economies of developing countries.

Yet the significance of the resolution of the oil crisis in the Middle East is that some redress of the imbalance may need to be granted if the dominant position of U.S. corporations within the raw-materials-producing countries is to be maintained.

Within the United States, the slower rates of growth have spelled higher levels of joblessness. After a long pause produced by the ebullient war economy of the 1960s official unemployment rates now exceed 5 percent regularly and the tendency for unemployment to increase seems chronic unless factors that will increase the overall pace of investment can overcome the trend. Until now, only substantial war preparations and increases in services employment have been able to reverse the trend since the 1950s.

Among the new features of the current economy is that defense spending is not declining in absolute terms—it is actually rising. But it is not keeping pace with the total production of goods and services so that its impact as a job-producing program has been considerably lessened. The recent moves of the Nixon administration to increase the war budget reflect both the political strength of the industries most intimately associated with this sector and the persistence of this form of wasteful investment as a recession-fighting tool.

Even the increased size of investments that occurred in 1973-1974 was not able to overcome the countervailing trend toward inflation and unemployment. New investments in the domestic steel industry are directed toward overcoming the technological backwardness of much of that industry. Similarly, machine-tool manufacturers are beginning to employ computerized lathes and other machine tools in the production process. The long-term effect of these developments is bound to be both labor and capital saving. Already the size of the steel labor force is declining even though output remains on a rising curve. The high prices of raw materials and machinery are only peripherally connected with rising fuel costs. More importantly, they reflect the growing concentration of ownership within these industries and the dominant position of the United States within this capital-producing sector.

Thus, slower growth rates combined with some technological change are responsible for the employment troubles at home. In turn, the merger movement of large corporations and tottering smaller businesses has accelerated over the past several years. This may not signal the end of competition in the narrow sense. Small businesses may continue to occupy the marginal niches within the marketplace, particularly in services of some aspects of the retail and wholesale trades.

But the small manufacturer is a dying breed, just as the small farmer is no more than a vestige of earlier times. There are few industries remaining for the entrance of small business. Even the old competitive groups such as textiles and clothing are increasingly becoming part of the conglomerate phenomenon. Such corporations as Genesco, ITT, Tenneco and Gulf + Western boast holdings in industries ranging from primary metals and chemicals to car leasing. The old services that were the province of the small-business are now owned by giant corporations that make decisions regarding their existence based purely on whether they can yield a rate of profit competitive with its other holdings. The calculation becomes entirely removed from sentiment, or even competition within the industry itself. If car leasing is more profitable than milk-processing, the latter is simply dropped in the conglomerate portfolio.

All these developments have meant that the historic pattern of consumption as well as production within the United States are being reversed. The most important feature of the past several years is the dramatic increase in the proportion of the income of working class people spent on food, clothing, shelter in comparison to other forms of expenditures. Contrary to estimates that purported to show that workers spent only 15 percent of their income on food throughout the late 1950s and 1960s, the 1970s has shown that food alone now accounts for as much as 30 percent of family incomes and rent has climbed to nearly 35 percent of income in many places. It may be that the earlier estimates were understated in order to demonstrate the feasibility of a high level of durable goods consumption; yet the rise in the proportion of income spent for food and shelter in the past two years is undeniable.

Clothing prices have been rising in part because of the high cost of agricultural commodities and synthetic materials which are oil derivatives and also because of the decline of the garment industry as a sector characterized by competition. The merger movement in the garment industries is no less powerful than in any of the heavier industries. A similar pattern is emerging in this industry to that of other economic sectors that have been taken over by conglomerates. Of course, another important influence on concentration of ownership in the clothing industry is the development of a more uniform type of clothing among men and women. The factor of product innovation, called style in the production of clothing, has not vanished; but it has been reduced as an important factor maintaining a high degree of competition within it. The growth of informal clothing, particularly jeans and other leisure-wear for all types of use, has facilitated the growth of very large units in the industry. The key in clothing manufacturing is not so much a high level of capital investment, although there has been some growth of new production technologies in the industry. Rather, capital is required for high-powered marketing such as the employment of a large sales force, big advertising campaigns and other promotional activities. The expansion of such companies as Haggar, Henry I. Siegel, Levi-Strauss, Lee, in the mass leisure-wear industry is a reflection of the trend toward bigness in the midst of the simplification of men's styles. These corporations have departed from the old practice of producing a single garment such as pants. HIS produces an entire line of men's leisure-wear, either directly in its own plants or by contracting out to other companies.

The convergence of men's and women's leisure styles and the end of formal wear has also become an important means of enhancing concentration of ownership and market control by a few large companies. The Cluett Peabody, Manhattan Shirt and Van Heusen companies have established dominance over the shirt industry, both for men and women, paralleling the extension of concentrated power in the leisure-wear industry. Among women's wear, Bobbie Brooks and Jonathan Logan among others have captured positions of overwhelming importance in an industry marked by extreme competition until the 1950s. Underlying the growth of these companies, in turn, are the large investments by banks and holding companies in the clothing industry.

The proliferation of marketing costs is passed on to the price of clothing so that direct production costs are only one important determinant of price. The small manufacturer is losing his traditional importance in the clothing industry and the "contractor" wholly dependent on the large corporation has become the characteristic small-business person in the clothing trades. These contractors are in no way to be confused with entrepreneurship. They are little more than plant managers for the corporations and possess no genuine independence.

Housing starts, once a bellwether of economic activity, have slipped badly in the 1970s. The inflated prices of new housing, attributable to the high cost of credit as much as the increased costs of production, have discouraged working class people from purchasing new houses. After World War II the capacity of the economy to reconvert from war to peacetime production was facilitated by a high level of demand for new housing. The need is still desperate not only because large portions of older housing within the cities are badly deteriorated, but because the quality of postwar single- or two-family houses was so poor that they need replacement after only twenty-five or thirty years.

The credit system has been badly strained by the rising costs of food, clothing and transportation. Although there is plenty of money available for all types of large investments, the rate of interest has systematically discouraged both small business and the purchase of consumer durables. High interest rates for personal consumption have been an important factor restraining buying in automobiles, appliances and other durable goods. But more important than the inflated credit system for discouraging consumption has been the percentages required for purchase of such necessities as food, fuel and clothing in comparison to the durables. The food and energy crises have raised sharply the problem of how the American economy will survive in the light of this seemingly long-range reversal. It appears quite certain that the level of buying for consumer durables will not recover significantly in the near future and that the cutbacks of production and employment in these industries may be permanent. There is no observable tendency for a concomitant reduction in auto, appliances or home prices. The internal structural features of these industries show a fairly rigid price mechanism governed by the requirements of the profit rate. Given the probability of declining sales there is every reason to believe that prices are likely to increase, rather than be reduced in response to weakening demand. This tendency was made explicit in 1974 by the Consolidated Edison Company (ConEd) in New York which announced its need for a price increase because of reduced demand for services. Similarly, the Ford and Chrysler corporations raised prices on 1975 models despite a sharp sales drop in 1974. Under conditions of oligopolistic control of production and distribution, the tendency for prices to rise despite sagging demand indicates an historic reversal of classical competitive economic laws. In the public utilities this reversal has been elevated to an argument for price increases.

IV

The trouble with the foregoing scenario is that the working class has not been conditioned to expect hardship. Rather, the last several generations of workers have been sold on the idea that, whatever its faults, at least the United States provided for the material needs of most people. The central feature by which this country legitimates the entire social system is its capacity to "deliver the goods." Americans have been raised on the idea that food, clothing and shelter can be taken for granted. Even the automobile is part of the necessities of life. Moreover, there was every reason to believe that a new home, or at least a substantially recent model, can be expected as part of the wages of labor. In the past thirty years, the political economy of scarcity has been far removed from everyday consciousness. For example, the idea of spending most of the week's wages on the so-called material necessities with little left over for leisure, credit payments on durable goods, and a small amount of savings for future needs such as the kids' education or entrance into a small business, has been beyond the expectations of blue- and white-collar workers.

The central cultural and political question facing Americans today is whether they will accept that which is ordinary for many of their European counterparts: a life of hard times under almost all conditions. It is probable that the food and energy crises of 1973-1974 were preparations for a much longer term of downward adjustment in the standard of living. The ideological function of the liberal appeal for stoic acceptance of the new scarcity was to provide a moral argument for the decline of real wages and the deterioration of the quality of everyday life. But there is no reason, short of the belief that conditioning can produce any kind of persons desired by the programmers of human behavior, that Americans possess the moral and social fibre to readily accept the new lifestyle proposed by the government and its corporate masters.

The great lesson of the Vietnam war, for instance, was that patriotism could no longer be taken for granted. On the contrary, there is now every reason to assume that patriotic appeals are ineffective in enforcing industrial and social discipline. The drastic change in the political sensibility of the new generations of Americans is only partially attributable to the evaluation of the specific merits of the past war. More profoundly, the degree of skepticism of ordinary 'Americans about the patriotic claims of its government is related to what may be termed the "information" revolution. There is still a high degree of concealment in the reporting of news or the obfuscation in the reporting of public events. Yet there is sufficient dissemination of the violence and deceit that permeates diplomacy and other forms of politics as to raise serious questions about the justice of government appeals for loyalty among ordinary citizens against the external enemy.

To a great extent, democratic ideology is responsible for the emerging critical sensibilities of young and older Americans. The belief that the United States *ought* to stand for certain material achievements and moral principles within a democratic, open society generated the skeptical attitudes revealed during the Vietnam war. Besides, the myth of invincibility was sufficiently shattered during that war to raise questions about one of the crucial underpinnings of American patriotism. Battlefield defeats told only part of the story. More important was the seeming impossibility of ending the war after almost a decade of fighting. Neither the vaunted military power of the United States nor its immense economic resources were capable of ending the fighting, much less subduing the enemy.

Watergate and other "national disgraces" certainly have played an important role in shaking the confidence of most Americans in government and corporate appeals for sacrifice in the face of the impending shortages. To be sure, the characteristic reaction to the most recent skulduggery has been cynicism rather than mass anger. Yet, it has complicated the task of imposing a new material ethos on the nation. In past wars or depressions, an enemy was found to account for the malaise and facilitate the acceptance of scarcity. The austerity during World War II was accepted as a price paid for the defeat of fascism. In the same manner, Soviet communism was a sufficient reason for asking that Americans be prepared to die to save their material and spiritual culture after the war. It was difficult to find an adequate enemy during the Vietnam war precisely because of the closer ties that were being forged with the old Soviet enemy. The Soviet Union, we were constantly being told, was as interested in restoring peace in Southeast Asia as the United States. Even the old standby the "yellow peril" was more difficult to invoke. The Chinese were giving American ideologists few weapons to use in the futile attempt to mobilize the American people for wartime fervor. They were said to be cautious in their support of the Vietnamese Communists. They were portrayed as a nation busily engaged in solving its own pressing problems, leaving little energy and few resources to provide massive aid to their ostensible allies.

As for the North Vietnamese themselves, it was difficult to convince the American people of their brutality, always an important tool to whip up popular war fever. They were a smaller nation, primarily agricultural rather than industrial, and boasted a worldwide reputation for indefatigable heroic struggle against a succession of invaders. Despite some censorship, the American press frankly reported many appealing aspects of Vietnamese life. Even in the south, there was considerable dissension against the repressive regimes sponsored by the United States. Some non-Communist forces were as adamant in their opposition to the invasion by American troops as were the North Vietnamese.

In large measure, therefore, the United States has confronted its crisis of legitimacy simultaneously with its economic woes. This conjuncture raises substantial doubts about the political outcome of the present economic crisis whose resolution must be sought amid widespread anger and distrust of the whole political and social structure.

Of course, the dissent has deeper roots than either the broad dissemination of the facts of corruption in high places or the denouement of masses regarding patriotic appeals by a government whose own credibility seems subject to constant doubt. Beyond these are two other issues: the psychological effects of the challenge to the presumption of American affluence as a permanent feature of American consciousness and the decline in real living standards that had preceded the crisis. It will be no easy task to persuade most working people that high wages, which were the past motive for their acceptance of alienating and often arduous labor, must be forfeited to preserve the eminent economic and political status of multinational corporations. Such persuasion is beyond the powers of those who control American economic life. The erstwhile successes of wartime appeals for sacrifice were, in no small measure, due to the ability of the American economic system to deliver relatively full employment and increased real wages for many. If boring, mindless work were to be accepted, the promise of a more tolerable leisure life had to be delivered.

This is no longer within the immediate range of the American system. And herein lies the difficulty of the coming period. The economic basis of the moral appeal has been removed and the moral appeal has itself suffered eclipse. The second problem in terms of a smooth readjustment in the expectations of most working class Americans is that the legitimating institutions that have served well to maintain industrial discipline and the other prerequisites of social cohesion are also in the process of decline. The claim of schools to provide the reality of mobility has been severely shaken during the economic slowdown. In recent years, it has become abundantly evident that the success of schooling as an instrument for lateral, much less upward, mobility is entirely dependent on the singular factor of economic growth. Otherwise, mobility is reserved for the "best and the brightest" but the ability of public education to hold its participants for long periods has been eroded. Economic stagnation has been largely responsible for declining enrollments in public institutions of higher learning. In response, we are witnessing a widespread tendency toward the downgrading of the liberal arts curriculum, which is now judged practically useless.

American educational ideology is undergoing a substantial change to accommodate itself to the requirements of the social system. As the requirements for all kinds of scientific and intellectual workers decline in the economy as a whole, the need for technicians increases. The change from one type of "brain worker" to a downgraded brain worker has several roots: first, the slowing of product innovation as a thrust of research and development activities and increased emphasis on efficiency and quality control requiring technical labor of reduced intellectual level. Second, especially in the human services, the fiscal crisis has produced the demand for the replacement of highly credentialed professionals with paraprofessionals trained by community colleges. Third, the general diminution in job opportunities for teachers at all levels of the educational system has reduced the social basis for the maintenance of a liberal arts emphasis.

American educational theory now emphasizes the economizing benefits of programmed learning that allow individual students to work at their own pace without the constant supervision of a teacher. Such techniques as visual and oral aids, mechanical and segmented learning, and unit skills are combined with an emphasis on reading and math skills to the virtual exclusion of sciences, social sciences and humanities as the heart of the curriculum. "Open" learning that allows students to select courses without prerequisites or the need to fulfill minimum conditions of languages and the sciences is becoming more common in colleges and high schools. Even reading and math courses are related to putative job functions and have de-emphasized the theoretical content of these disciplines.

The struggle of parents and some educators on behalf of traditional types of schooling can be explained as a reaction to this trend toward the transformation of education into training. To be sure, the demand for "skills" by parents seems to be fulfilled by high-powered, machine-oriented reading programs. But, beneath the renewed interest by educational institutions in skills development is the deep belief that intellectual development is bound to lead to discontent on the part of the students if jobs are not demanding enough to use this type of educational experience.

Higher education is becoming vocational in theory as well as practice in most state and municipal schools. Facing stiffer competition for jobs than at any time since the Depression, students are now being offered course sequences purporting to provide specific, specialized skills leading to direct employment rather than a broad conceptual curriculum designed to provide the tools of mobility.

The expectations of students are being simultaneously lowered and raised in schools. The dreams of high-paying, prestigious and interesting work that is said to accrue from the attainment of various college degrees are shattered. At the same time, however, college is expected to yield concrete results in the job market. Of course, the school as a training ground for specific jobs has always been a highly dubious enterprise and remains so despite the introduction of vocational courses on a mass scale.

Many students enter colleges with the expectation that they will receive training rather than education to prepare them for the job market. But the dropout rate remains high, especially when students learn that the occupational payoff of their efforts is chimerical or that the pressures of earning a living now do not justify remaining in school for objectives that seem less inviting than they were led to believe. The recent drop of enrollments among entering freshmen as well as other levels of college students over the past several years has increased the fiscal problems of many schools. But it is also a sign of diminished influence of the colleges and universities on young adults. There can be no doubt that some of the aura that has surrounded higher schooling has been removed by the new vocational emphasis of state-supported schools. Even those attending private colleges, traditionally considered the training grounds of the elite and the alleged repositories of the "Western tradition," have lost their zeal for enduring the routines and rituals associated with initation rites into managerial and professional roles. Beyond the student disillusionment produced by the tightening job market for most professions or the higher tuition costs, the elite schools face the problem of capitalist society as a whole: the reduced legitimacy of the tenets of "Western" ideology and morality. For many, the virtue of safeguarding the vaults of the accumulated wisdom of the Western World is not at all clear. There have been too many wars, too much malfeasance in high office, too much evidence that the corporate conscience is nothing more than another handout of their public relations departments. Managing the empire seems less attractive in proportion to the discovery that the United States represents no higher example for the world to follow.

The growing tendency of students in elite schools to define their objectives in purely vocational terms does not have the same significance as it does for their counterparts in state schools. The expanding enrollments in law and medical schools and the concomitant decline of interest in science, humanities and social science may be attributed, in a great measure, to the drying up of many professional opportunities, particularly teaching and scientific research. But the problem goes much deeper.[1] Students leave graduate schools without having profoundly internalized the belief system necessary for corporate survival. The old ideologies of pluralism according to which the United States is a whirling dervish of pressure groups contending for political and social power has given way to a widely accepted belief that a few powerful economic groups have effectively foreclosed the possibility of a broad distribution of power among the masses.

The popularity of the notion of the power elite is by no means an indication that Marxist theory pervades the university. On the contrary. What has occurred instead is the spread of a heavy pall of cynicism among graduate students and those who attend private elite schools. They may enter the corporate or government bureaucracies but lack fervor for their work. Their confidence in the transmitted ideas is severely shaken, although most have not opted to remain beyond the pale of public and business institutions.

The crisis of legitimacy is the product of the historical developments of the last decade. Young people began the Kennedy era with high hopes that the American hegemony would mean peace and abundance for the whole world. The disillusionment with the Peace Corps, the assassination of the Kennedys and of Martin Luther King, Jr. the overt injustice of the Vietnam war, and the apparent reduction of the United States to a second-class economic power in the 1970s all contributed to the manifest break between youth and the social system. Yet, in the last analysis, the most important factor serving to loosen the affiliation of young people with corporate society was the collapse of the liberal wing of the Democratic Party after its crushing defeats of 1968 and 1972. It was not so much that the "progressives" lost at the Democratic Convention in 1968 or the election four years later, that produced the "apolitical" and weary syndrome among middle class youth. It was more the atmosphere of resignation that enveloped the liberal camp after the Nixon triumphs.

Among the most dramatic examples of the collapse and resignation of the liberal wing was the retreat by Senator Edward Kennedy from his bill to establish a national health insurance and the adoption of a compromise measure that sacrificed both the comprehensiveness of the legislation and its independence from business interests. The only significant liberal congressional victory was raising the minimum wage in 1974 to $2 an hour, a measure that was originally enacted three years earlier. By the time the bill became law, and a badly battered President Nixon was forced to sign it, it had already become obsolete as a significant way to increase living standards.

In my view, the felt impotence of American liberalism is only a reflection of the death of the last vestiges of national capitalism that sustained the pluralistic myths for a half-century beyond its reality. The concentration of corporate power to an unprecedented degree since the end of the 1960s has proved much too powerful a force for those seeking to restore the forms of competitive enterprise or to assert the hegemony of the middle class in American political life. George McGovern's victory within the Democratic Party was a defeat for the older Democratic, middle class-based politics, a sign of the breakup of the city as the decisive force in national politics.

George McGovern received 37 percent of the popular vote, only 1 percent less than Hubert Humphrey's percentage in his 1968 bid for the presidency. Richard Nixon's overwhelming victory in 1972 is partly attributable to his capturing George Wallace's constituency, which had traditionally been associated with the Democratic Party. Many blue collar workers voted for Nixon because they felt that McGovern remained loyal to the old welfare policies of the New Deal, Fair Deal, and New Frontier. These policies are still attractive to some of the old Democratic constituency, mostly the blacks and the poor. But working people were no longer interested in the enlargement of government power that McGovern's programs promised. Instead they were mainly concerned with the decline of their real wage, which has been exacerbated by increasingly higher taxes needed to pay for such government programs.

v

The middle class of small businessmen and independent professionals could not be expected to carry the burden of the struggle against big capital. They represent neither the most decisive social forces capable of mounting a counterattack nor the adequate ideologies for conducting the struggle. The former weakness has been evident for many years. The novel feature of the current situation is the revelation that the old base of democratic reform within the working class is in the process of disintegrating. The reliability of the working class as a subordinate ally of the Democratic liberal wing in the arena of electoral politics was substantially called into question

during the past two national elections even as those workers who cast their ballots for Nixon remained loyal to the
Democratic congressional delegations throughout the
country.

The "genteel populism" of Ralph Nader and other
modern day muckrakers has failed to capture the imagination of the workers. Its relentless attack on "bigness"
and corruption seems curiously discordant with the mild
flavor of proposals to expand government regulation of
business abuses. Most ludicrous was the proposal to
co-opt public members on the boards of large corporations. The demand for inclusion was seen as no more than
a type of acceptance of corporate capitalism despite the
condemnatory rhetoric that dominates the work of the
Nader group. At best Nader has provided the outlines of
a program for a middle class populism. Its result may
belie its intentions, however. Designed to curb the rampant power of capital, the programs of legislative and corporate reform may institutionalize the very system against
which the valuable reports and exposé of Nader's Raiders
is directed.

Rightwing populism has had a much deeper effect on
working class consciousness. It speaks to the fears of
white workers who realize the tenuousness of their job security. It may be that the incipient alliance of the black
middle class with corporate leaders, combined with job
insecurity, is far more important as an explanation for the
receptivity of white workers to the appeals of the George
Wallaces than any other factor. The black middle class is
not a middle class in the classic meaning of the term;
there are still very few black entrepreneurs. The new
black middle class consists of professional people, such as
teachers and ministers, and administrators created by
government programs such as anti-poverty and by corporate efforts to find black supervisors among their labor

force. The new stratum of black administrators represents a significant force in black neighborhoods even though its numbers are relatively small.

The importance of the black middle class stems from its visibility, especially its participation in corporate liberal efforts to eradicate poverty and unemployment. Many white workers view this alliance with distrust, forgetting that the overwhelming majority of black people in the United States are workers and therefore do not share in the benefits of corporate-sponsored programs, which are aimed at the ghetto. Nevertheless, such organizations as the Urban Coalition and the National Alliance of Businessmen that represent the coalition of the black middle class with the large corporations become grist for the demagoguery of rightwing populists.

In a number of cities, such as Atlanta, Newark, Cleveland and Los Angeles, members of this new black middle class have been elected mayor with more or less overt support of corporate philanthropic organizations. In the city of Philadelphia, on the other hand, Frank Rizzo, the conservative policeman, was able to make a political issue of this alliance and win support of a substantial number of working class white voters.

Moreover, unlike the leftist liberals whose attack against big business is accompanied by a call for more government intervention that implies the enlargement of the bureaucracy, the rightwing opponents of big government attack the bureaucracy itself as a central evil. The daily experience of working class people confirms the pejorative connotations to the concept of bureaucracy. In their lives, corporate and trade union bureaucracies are viewed as obstacles to the fulfillment of their needs—if not outright enemies. Contrary to the popular support enjoyed by the New Deal, which represented an historical watershed in the maturation of bureaucratic domination in the United States, latter day proponents of welfarism and other centralist means to alleviate economic want face the opposition of large segments of working people, as much as a considerable group of corporations who are only willing to support increased government spending in the war sector.

The motivation for worker opposition to enlarged government spending and social programs has a material base in the back-breaking tax burden upon them that resulted from the massive intervention by the state in the national economy during the Depression. We have had three decades of relatively full employment during which workers have realized that their contributions are the main sources of public spending. The reaction against new welfare programs takes the appearance of virulent opposition to the demands of racial minorities. However, its roots lie in the simultaneous heavy tax burden and inflationary spiral. To the extent that the core liberal program is still grounded in the old appeal to the enlargement of the welfare state, to that extent its base among the working class has diminished.

What is remarkable about the present situation is that, despite a sluggish economy, there seems little legislative impetus for enacting a massive tax cut to stimulate economic activity. Instead, the 1970s have witnessed the imposition of a plethora of new, regressive taxes. State and local sales taxes have risen. Highway-use taxes, especially in the northeast, have doubled in some instances. And, most insidious, a new form of taxation has been introduced—the gambling tax and the lottery. Since poor people are among the heaviest gamblers, the levelling of a tax on these winnings is particularly discriminatory against the small bettor. The paradox of government policy is that legalized gambling is becoming more and more a tool for revenue creating and, at the same time, a way to take a double bite out of income.

There is another important source of popular opposition to all kinds of traditional solutions to the crisis. Among the central features of the past decade is the emergence of an "incompletely socialized" individual. This person is by no means convinced that any form of electoral activity, particularly on the national level, is worth the trouble of participation. The phenomenon of the abstaining voter has reached alarming proportions in America, at least compared to European countries.

In the 1972 elections nearly forty-four million persons of voting age stayed home from the polls. This group was larger than the vote received by the Democratic Party's standard bearer and represented more than one-third of the potential electorate. Abstention took two forms: many of those who registered failed to vote. But an even larger number refused to register. This trend was marked among first voters, particularly the eighteen-to-twenty-year-old group who were made eligible for the first time to vote in a national election by a constitutional amendment.

Among the conventional explanations for the failure of youth to take advantage of their franchise in 1972 was that the Democratic Party standard bearer, George McGovern, was unable to capture the imagination of this potentially progressive constituency. A more dynamic campaign, especially a platform that spoke to the new cultural needs of the young people, such as abortion reform, a liberalized drug law, a more radical civil rights program and new initiatives against the war budget, may have spelled a different result, so the argument runs. Other contentions seem closer to the truth. Despite specific platform deficiencies, the main problem of McGovern's image was that his differences with Nixon narrowed as the campaign wore on. He became more cautious about striking out in bold new directions, but the boldest break with Nixon would have had to be on the central issue of bureaucratic and antiauthoritarian forms of national government, including the power of the executive branch itself.

Beyond the problems associated with the strategy of the Democratic Presidential campaign remains the essential question of antielectoral impulses among youth. Just as the candidates were perceived as fundamentally similar, young people suspect that all politicians are alike and that any who may be qualitatively different are destined for either assassination or obscurity. Beneath these judgments is the sense that to be "apolitical" is the proper response to the charade of national elections. Here the term apolitical should not be understood as apathy. True, youth in the 1970s have shown a propensity to build their houses and chop their wood and make their gardens grow, in the words of the final scene of *Candide*. But privatization should not be interpreted as more than an expression of contempt for the public forum which seems so completely monopolized by political and cultural figures devoted to the conventional wisdom. Young workers and students who have taken their leave of demonstrations, electoral struggles and other typical arenas of approved protest, are more conscious of the reality of corporate domination of American life than ever before. They have lost faith in the traditional appeals and, unlike their predecessors of the 1960s are not convinced that small measures can alter the situation.

The impulse to reject ordinary avenues of opposition has not found its own organizational expression. The new Stalinist left, distinguished from its own forebears by no more than longer hair and informal attire but similar in almost all other respects, is decidedly unattractive to radicalized and depoliticized youth. Rather, the young evince an intense concern with the vagaries of private life. It is not so much the search for careers that impels many to return to school, or to pay more attention to their jobs. It is the tighter job market on one hand and the disappearance of any centers of sensible political opposition on the other that have produced a new interest in work as a goal. This emphasis is not antipolitical, however. It has produced new conditions for political struggle. Many young people define their politics in terms of their vocational and personal choices rather than the rituals of public activity. The questions of marriage and the family, sexuality and child-rearing, and other aspects of interpersonal relations have been transformed from a suppressed issue into a central focus of social consciousness. In part, the new politics of everyday life resulted from the insight that knee-jerk responses to the prevailing alienated framework in which public life has been constricted, is itself an alienating activity. But beyond the purely reactive reasons for the shift lay the recognition that these needs can no longer be deferred, that the personal is the political, that something can be done in this sphere in contrast to the helplessness one individual or a small group feels about the larger public issues of the energy crisis or the inflationary tendencies of the economy as a whole.

VI

The search for a framework for the development of an opposition to the centralization of power in the United States inevitably poses the question of whether the trade union movement is likely to emerge as a center of mass opposition to the large multinational corporations. Beyond the liberal and socialist traditions of some unions, particularly their consistent record on behalf of such reforms as social welfare, civil rights legislation, national health insurance, and labor's own right to organize and bargain collectively with employers as a matter of law, the union movement is more specifically self-interested in the implications of the food and energy crises and the larger purview of the power of the multinational corporations.

First, the combined crises have materially affected the living standards of union members. In prior periods organized workers were able to win concessions from the large corporations in those industries having a high degree of vertical integration or at least where the manufacturer controlled much of the marketing operations despite decentralized control of retailing itself. However, the new inflationary conditions, the sporadic shortages in essential commodities, and the shift in the pattern of worker consumption have blocked many avenues that were formerly available for protecting real wages. The major tool currently employed by trade unions to protect real wages is the provision of cost of living increases. They are a supplement to periodic wage hikes but have upper limits beyond which the employer is not obliged to go. The so-called "escalator clauses," which tie a portion of wages to the consumer price index, are woefully inadequate to help workers weather the torrential inflation currently afflicting the American economy.

Nor is the garden variety collective bargaining agreement able to deal with a second important consequence of current economic trends—the international runaway shop. Virtually no union agreements protect members against plant removal except in terms of its impact—through such devices as pensions, and, in some cases, supplementary unemployment benefits. In steel and auto, the companies are required to supplement state unemployment benefits for a period of a year. But provisions such as vesting rights for pensions and supplementary unemployment benefits assume a return to full employment after a term or some stability in other sectors of the industry that would make valuable employer and worker contributions to pension plans even after termination of employment in a particular location. The consequences of the removal of plants from the United States to other countries are much deeper than the removal of plants from one part of the United States to another. Workers may receive transfer options in collective agreements, but there are no provisions within the contract for international transfer. Nor is there ordinarily the desire for such rights either by managers or by the workers themselves.

Despite the downward movement of production in the United States over the past several years (production actually declined in the first quarter of 1974 by almost 6 percent, the worst drop in sixteen years[2]), unions have evinced only marginal interest in developing a self-interested program for protecting jobs. The exceptions to the rule are the textile and needle trades that have evolved a protectionist policy with respect to foreign competition. The union label campaigns of the Amalgamated Clothing Workers, International Ladies Garment Workers Union and the import quota proposals advanced by the Textile Workers Union, are defensive actions oriented to a narrow approach to the problem of the fact that lower wage areas of Europe, Asia and the Caribbean have undercut the industry within the United States.

On the whole, these campaigns have slowed, but have by no means halted the exodus of portions of the garment industries to other parts of the world. Beyond wage competition, among the reasons for the successful emergence of other countries as major clothing producers is the higher degree of capital concentration in consumer good industries abroad. Garment plants are ordinarily larger in Europe than their United States counterparts. The extent of technological development is far superior in some respects and, most important, textile and clothing plants in such countries as Italy and Spain are vertically integrated. In sum, these goods can be offered at substantially cheaper prices than United States-made products. This phenomenon extends to the shoe industry, which has removed in a great measure from the United States to Spain, North Africa and parts of Southeast Asia. In the 1970s it is painfully obvious that the traditional consumer goods industries within the United States are destined for an accelerated downslide, despite the best efforts of the unions. Compounding the problem, the textile workers and shoe workers unions are small and weak; nearly 80 percent of the cotton branches of the industry remains unorganized, and a similar proportion of shoe manufacturing within the United States remains nonunion.

The textile industry is a case study of the beginning of the end of the advantages of unionized workers to those who have not joined unions and more profoundly, the international leveling of wages between Western capitalist countries. Besides trying to hold its important position within the synthetic fibers and dyeing industries, TWUA has concentrated most of its efforts to curb imports and to agitate for raising the wages of nonunion sectors of its jurisdiction in order to safeguard its members' jobs in wool and cotton. But wages among United States textile workers, already low by American standards, are already beginning to be matched by wages of West Germany, French and British workers in terms of real buying power.

The problems in steel, auto construction and other major industries are not the same as those in so-called soft, consumer goods industries. In these industries, the central issues affecting job security are those of plant relocation to other countries by major corporations based within the United States and technological, job-destroy-ing changes, both of which result in permanent layoffs. The steel industry in particular has moved within recent years to replace a good portion of its older plant and equipment by computer-controlled machines. The parts plants of the auto industry have been similarly mechanized and new orders for machines for overseas plants have been filled by the machine-tool producing manufacturers using an ever-increasing proportion of automatic equipment.

The characteristic response of the trade unions in these industries has been to accept technological change as a progressive development of ultimate benefit to their membership. New machines have created more work for skilled trade union workers, and have reduced the numbers of structural oppositionists—the blacks, youth and women, who occupy the unskilled and semi-skilled jobs. Higher technologies require a greater portion of installers, machine repair workers, tool and die and pattern makers and construction crafts, and fewer unskilled workers. The United Auto Workers accepted the permanent reduction of the work force in the industry by 80,000 without a murmur. From the union's perspective, the General Motors, Ford and Chrysler corporations still have the right to determine the number of workers needed in relation to the quantity of production within the limits agreed to by the contract. After thirty-five years of auto unionism, there is as yet no force within the union asking that management prerogatives to hire and fire on a mass scale be controlled by criteria other than profit.

The Steelworkers union, which, together with the Auto Workers, is the largest within American manufacturing industries, has shown similar indifference to the pace and intensity of technological change. The issue of foreign competition seems temporarily suppressed in the wake of a large backlog of orders for all kinds of steel. But productivity is taking significant leaps in the industry and only the higher levels of production have prevented a substantial reduction in the work force.

Many jobs in the auto industry are moving to other places. The Union's rhetorical understanding of the need for international cooperation among trade unions to exercise some restraint on the activities of the multinational corporations has not been matched by practical steps. To a great extent, the American trade unions remain narrow, nationally oriented unions in an international economy. Neither the International Federations established within each industry nor the International Confederation of Free Trade Unions nor its Communist led counterpart, the World Federation of Trade Unions, have shown any inclination to initiate actions designed to halt or control the free movement of plants and jobs. They have remained content with hand wringing, revealing the shortness of their vision.

On a broader front, the trade unions have become, more than ever, the guardians of the traditional social order. They show no signs of departing from this position, despite the periodic outbursts of leaders of the AFL-CIO, the Auto Workers and the Teamsters against the national administration and its policies. In 1973, the president of the Labor Federation, George Meany, actually became a proponent of the impeachment of Richard Nixon and the AFL-CIO executive council and convention delegates enthusiastically concurred in the call for the ouster of the errant President. What is remarkable about these actions is that they were followed up with almost no public action by union members themselves. Even in those parts of the labor movement where the leadership claims a loyal following, labor's legions were not marshaled to pressure Congress, demonstrate against the administration nor mobilize rank and file members to support the leadership's program. The calm surrounding the AFL-CIO's revolt against the administration after a long period of friendly neutrality gave pause to those who would welcome signs of resistance by the trade union hierarchy against the policies of the corporations and their government allies. The meager result flowing from labor's brief moment of honor can only add to the belief that the trade unions will only watch passively the new offensives of the international capitalists.

VII

The collapse of American liberalism, the disaffection of the trade unions from liberals and their subsequent hunger for respectability and accommodation with the largest corporations and the end of the overt phase of the youth revolt, leaves only scattered visible signs of opposition to the policies of the oil companies, the food monopolies and the government that coordinates and regulates their dominant position in the world.

That opposition is not confined to the women's movement, groups of individuals, hard-core environmentalists and consumer vanguards who have rejected the notion of scarcity as a virtue. The revolt is also evident among workers who have not followed their unions into the accommodating ideology of labor management cooperation for 1974. When the Steelworkers' union and the United States Steel Corporation responded to the crisis by making an agreement that replaced the strike weapon with arbitration and retained a "sensible" wage increase of about 5 percent a year, this deal was met with considerable rank and file displeasure. Among the forms of opposition was the candidacy of a rank and file member of the union in its biggest district, the Chicago-Gary area. The campaign was closely fought and the rank and file movement nearly succeeded in defeating the administration. Simultaneously a group of rank and file steelworkers filed a suit in federal court to prevent the company and the union from putting the no-strike agreement into effect. The union, in an effort to persuade the rank and file to accept the agreement, actually used the threat of international competition, the recent history of technological backwardness in the industry and the desire for benefits to aid the older workers as arguments for abandoning the strike weapon. The arbitration procedure, it claimed, would enable the company and the union to plan more carefully to save the industry. Higher profits were needed by the companies to meet the competition abroad by modernization. Thus, workers should not demand wage increases beyond reasonable guide lines.

The steel settlement is only the most extreme form of tendencies emerging through the labor movement toward closer cooperation with companies. Traditionally militant unions such as the Electrical workers coalition that conducted a prolonged and pathbreaking strike against GE and Westinghouse in 1970 settled their contract in 1974 peacefully without establishing any new breakthroughs in wages or the control over working conditions. Similarly, the settlement between the UAW and the big three auto companies in 1973 was marked by modest provisions. In addition, the union was found to have made a "backdoor" agreement with the Ford Motor Company regarding overtime regulations for skilled workers. In a union long boasting a rigorous observance of democratic processes, this revelation had the impact of a scandal. Moreover, just prior to the contract settlement, the leadership employed goons in some plants to smash wildcat strikes and other illegal protests initiated by the rank and file. In the process, however, the distance between the leadership and the membership widens. In some cases, the unions have surrendered their traditional opposition to tying wages to productivity, and have gone along with speedup programs that result in serious occupational health and safety hazards. These accommodations have become particularly onerous to rank and file union members, especially those working under particularly dangerous conditions. The refusal of workers to surrender their hard-won working conditions or to accept prevailing hazardous work was a fundamental impulse behind the overturn of the Boyle administration in the United Mine Workers and the election of a rank and file slate. Returning war veterans and school graduates found their only jobs in the coal mines. This development lowered the average age of working miners for the first time in two generations and was a social basis for the raised level of discontent within the industry. The old leadership was not rejected primarily on the issue of its proven corruption, although this feature played a significant role in the rise of the opposition movement. The change of leadership was the direct result of the desire by working miners for a democratic union that would militantly reflect its interests and the refusal to accept the inevitability of death and disease as the price of higher miners' wages.

Even after the electoral victory of the new administration, wildcat strikes broke out in West Virginia and Eastern Kentucky, the nation's major coal regions. These strikes were signs that worker militancy had not subsided after the new officers took over the union and that workers were not willing to wait for the contract negotiations or the grievance procedure to solve their problems.

Among the angriest of all workers are public employees. The major implication of the new dimensions of corporate power for the public sector has been to reduce its services to the point where the characterization of the public sector as a "poorhouse" state has become appropriate. The fiscal crisis of the state is a direct result of the historic decision to finance public services as well as all other functions of government out of wages and salaries. The proliferation of administration in the society as a whole took place with a vengeance within the public sector. Every level of government increased employment in the 1950s and 1960s. But with the slackening of economic growth, the country faced a conflict of priorities. Consequently, the government attempted to resolve the struggle between those costs directly attributable to the provision of corporate needs and those required by the poor, the aged and others almost entirely dependent on the state, by the relative impoverishment of the welfare sector. The shrunken base of government income was compensated by skyrocketing taxes, demands on workers for accelerated productivity and a firmer attitude toward wage increases.

Of all workers, the public employees have been among the least willing to yield their gains. Postal workers have rejected "realism" and appeals to patriotic or professional responsibility and have conducted mass strikes in recent years. As in the mines, the growing militancy of these workers is largely to be traced to the changing composition of the work force with respect to race, age and sex. Younger, black, and women workers are disenchanted with the efforts of union leaders to seek favors from Congress and the administration. Instead, they have gone the way of direct action, an unprecedented development among white collar workers, who have always been regarded as a pillar of society.

I do not wish to argue that these instances are characteristic of the working class as a whole, any more than the rise of movements for abortion and environmental reform are pervasive among the middle class. The pace of changes wrought by the crises over the past two years, combined with the general downturn in economic activity, have definitely taken the wind out of the sails of the revolts at the work place and in the consumer spheres. At the same time, it would be a mistake to try to claim that ordinary Americans endorse policies that have destroyed or set back environmental protections, eroded working conditions, or resulted in the deterioration of the living standards of most Americans. The crisis of legitimacy has deepened even if there has developed a substantial amount of cynicism about the chances for doing anything about social transformation.

# 5

# The Future of the American Dream

There is much cause for alarm. The revolt has many dimensions including the transformation of daily life. The evidence abounds that thousands of persons are embroiled in activities to transform their social relations, their working and their living environments, and their own consciousness. In my opinion, the struggle for self-liberation from the constraints imposed by the institutions charged with securing the political and social consent of the masses is an indispensable element in the revolutionary project.

The problem is that we have entered a period in which the concrete manifestation of the results of the revolution in daily life are still confined to the private sphere, while the elements of opposition in public activity are dominated by those who have failed to connect their politics with the psychic needs of the masses. Most Americans are still bound by the terms established by the corporate order. The preponderance of resistance remains en-

sconced within the private life, even though the public
intrudes into the private to an unprecedented degree and
social reality makes manifest the linkages.

The transformation of American capitalism is now becoming manifest. On one hand, the pluralistic myths are
no longer capable of sustaining the belief in the overall
rationality of the corporate system. The quantum leaps of
accumulated international wealth, control and power are
now so much a part of our ordinary lives, and permeate the
institutions of mass communication so completely, that
mass disaffection is almost a "given" of the political world.
On the other hand, this judgment implies that, at the
core, bourgeois rule is no longer sustained by ideology but
by the sheer exercise of power. The tolerance of political
opposition that was among the vaunted forms of social legitimation for the corporate order in the 1960s when its
economic problems seemed minuscule in the midst of
war-induced expansion have all but disappeared. There
can no longer be another Rosenberg case to occupy the
symbolic place needed to promulgate the psychology of
terror as in the 1950s. The enemy without is no longer
easily identified. It is now located within. The enemy
within is not an agent of a foreign power. It is as much
generalized terror as it is the organized forms of political
opposition. The corporate bourgeoisie desperately seeks
assent and senses resistance among the population at the
invisible crevices of daily life. Mass surveillance cannot be
justified on the basis of the old notions of Communist-
inspired subversion. Instead it rests on the pervasiveness
of criminality that is said to stalk the cities. It also has
new dimensions: the highjackers provided the impetus
for the growth of a whole new security force at airports.
Faded into memory are the feats of the daredevils of yes-
teryear who forced pilots to change their routes to exotic
places such as Cuba or Algiers. The electronic frisk no

longer needs an immediate justification. It has already been routinized as a fixture of air travel.

A new phenomenon that legitimizes the expansion of police forces and modern methods of mass surveillance is the political kidnaping, and murders of innocent citizens. In San Francisco in the Spring of 1974 a random group of whites were shot by a gang of black fanatics seeking revenge against their oppressors. The massive display of ultraviolet rays to detect criminals, the arbitrary police roundup of blacks in the city found their argument in the murders.

Mass fear may be said to have gripped large numbers of Americans. The walker in the city at night has become a rare person, scolded by friends and acquaintances for recklessness. For many, the streets have become alien ground—a potential source of death or a battlefield. The media pound home the lesson of incessant danger lurking in the everyday reality. Police harassment, once reserved for blacks and other minorities, has become so general as to affect every person.

The specter of criminal behavior lurking in every human person has replaced the ideological enemy. Instead of communism we have invented the evil within us all.

The forms of repression that have been employed to sustain the adherence of the mass of Americans to the complex maneuvers of the internationally involved large corporations have ranged from deliberate lying about the extent of that involvement to the surveillance of those who dare to doubt. American universities have been systematically shorn of dissenters, with the exception of some whose rebellion has been defined in terms of "cultural" issues such as women's liberation, black equality, and intellectual non-conformity. Even here, repressive tolerance has given way to outright repression. The number of teachers who have been fired from state-supported and private institutions of higher education has increased exponentially within the past few years. Added to the overall diminution of the academic marketplace has been the end of the brief affair between the liberal administration and the radicals. Once more, for radicals at least, the difficulty of finding a job is compounded by overt pressures for intellectual conformity. This tendency reveals the growing rigidity of the cultural institutions that as recently as the late 1960s welcomed token dissent among its employees.

Yet dissent is ineradicable despite the proliferations of surveillance activities, firings of dissenters, the end of "radical" themes in film, the difficulty experienced by many left-wing authors getting their work printed by magazines and book publishers.

Popular cynicism was reflected in the attitudes of the news media toward the energy and food crises. Nightly, television newscasts reported the refusal of ordinary people to accept the explanations for shortages and rising prices offered by the large oil corporations and the government. *The Wall Street Journal* (April 11, 1974) reported that some oil companies found that their advertising campaign in newspapers and on television was largely ineffective in explaining the high costs of fuel and bloated profit margins in terms of the need for expanded efforts to find new sources of oil and natural gas and alternative types of energy. Instead, the companies were finding that their own employees were better propagandists. Mobil Oil engineers and technicians were hitting the chicken and green peas circuit making the corporation's case. Women's clubs and service organizations were hearing of the oil company's woes from persons working on the "front line" of production and marketing.

The *Journal* found that listeners were still dubious. Despite the best efforts of public relations salespersons they suspected that the oil companies were making a giant profit grab at their expense. What is remarkable about these reports is that the statements of doubt were expressed by small-business people and professionals in smaller cities and towns who have been the historical bedrock of American ideology.

The apparent inability of the corporations to tell their story to a sympathetic audience raises some significant questions for the shape of things to come. There are no precedents since the Depression for a massive reduction of living standards in peacetime. Americans have been raised on the belief that economic expansion is a permanent feature of the corporate system. To be sure, there have been four recessions since the end of the Second World War. The decline of economic activity was relatively shortlived in all cases. In two instances (1949-1950, and 1960-1961), the major reasons for the revival of the economy were closely associated with a steep rise in defense expenditures. The 1954 and 1958 recessions were instances of the long-term stagnation that has afflicted the American economy since 1949 but was ended when a burst of new capital spending for the further mechanization of the steel, auto and chemical industries gave a major stimulus to economic growth.

The 1974 recession portends much more serious consequences. Compounding the chronic inability of the United States economy to sustain economic growth except under wartime conditions, is the realignment of the world system of production. The tendency toward the decentralization of industry on an international scale will affect the material living standards of American workers. Moreover, the days of cheap food and energy may be over so that even if a loose credit system can be maintained, working people may find that their incomes are simply insufficient to make new commitments to houses, cars and appliances. The large corporations in these industries are mostly multinational and have become conglomerates. Their pattern of capital investment overseas and into the most profitable sectors regardless of the impact on the internal and international economic situation has produced a serious imbalance in the American economy. In turn, the tendency toward investment in highly profitable service industries at the expense of the expansion and modernization of productive forces within the United States is narrowing the capital base of the United States economy. Contrary to the trend of the 1960s when the number of industrial jobs increased, especially in the war sector, the last year has witnessed a decline in factory employment and a slower rate of growth in the service sector. The structural distortion of the pattern of consumer spending resulting from the inflationary trend promises to further restrict capital spending in most consumer goods industries.

The rise of capital investment in the midst of the recession is as paradoxical from a traditional standpoint as it is revealing of the new configuration of economic life. Capital investment in modernization activities within the steel machine-tool industries at home and in consumer goods production overseas has been supplemented by a tremendous quantity of investment in service, retailing and other nonproductive sectors. This means that the classic inflationary situation has been built into the economy. The real basis of economic development, the production of commodities, is deteriorating within the United States, while a great deal of "spurious" capital formation is taking place, that is, capital that rests on the productive sector but is actually invested in services. For example, it is more profitable to invest in rental cars than in automobile production. Retailing is beginning to yield a relatively high rate of profit in comparison to former years when this industry was operating on very narrow profit margins. The point is that unless actual output of goods expands faster than the output of services the inflationary trend will continue and perhaps accelerate. Another example of this trend is that the heavy rate of investment in machinery, fertilizers, processing plants and other expansion of material goods are part of the maintenance of the basic productive forces of society. But, much of the investment is located in "futures"—speculative capital that banks on price increases, the consolidation of marketing and distribution into fewer hands, and other forms of nonproductive investment. This development means that more capital is chasing a highly restricted quantity of output of food because as the degree of concentration within the industry increases, the tendency is for a relative slowdown in production in order to keep prices high, and profits bountiful.

The reversal in the historical belief that profits are the outcome of high volume or mass production spells disruption for the ordinary processes of production and consumption. There will be frequent manipulated shortages of almost everything that is bought and sold. The notion that inflation can be stemmed by government action has one central defect—which is that the government is subject to the political domination of the large corporations. The penetration by corporations of government agencies charged with regulating business activity vitiates the idea that the state is separate from the marketplace and independent of ruling class control.

The transformation of the government into a direct instrument rather than a deterrent of price inflation is no more evident than in the agricultural sector where regulation has had an inflationary impact. Not only are prices kept high by direct government policies in terms of the size of agricultural output; as I have argued, the distribution of existing output between domestic and foreign consumption affects domestic prices. The use of farm products as a major source of export creates shortages. Prices are kept high by (1) retiring the land, or not planting crops, and/or (2) by diverting produce to overseas markets. The maintenance of a two-price system in cotton has now become a model for other agricultural commodities and has made inflation an aspect of government policy.

The shortages in raw materials in the agricultural and the industrial sectors are the outcome of the chronic weakness in the international trade position of the U.S. economy and the reluctance of U.S. corporations to undertake capital investment in primary raw materials development without substantial government subsidies. The problem with securing these subsidies is that federal financing has become the universal instrument for stabilizing economic activity. The private sector, particularly in highly concentrated industries, is simply beyond taking risks. Capital investment must be insured, supplemented and otherwise guaranteed by the state. The high degree of control exercised by the corporate sector over the state has removed the major source of inflation control.

There are no effective mechanisms for controlling inflation within a highly centralized and monopolistic economy. Nor are the American people likely to accept mass unemployment and the progressive decline of real wages without a struggle. The high cost of living has already depressed real wages to their 1965 levels in the past two years. Clearly, corporate and government decision-makers will be constrained to find some solutions to the crisis. I believe that the chance of stemming inflation depends entirely on finding ways to expand production of real goods. This option is foreclosed by the international commitments of United States corporations who hold the reigns of power. Their decision has been to expand investments in oil, consumer goods and information-related industries such as computers, in other countries. And there are good political and economic reasons for this direction of investment. Even China is likely to become a recipient of development capital. Certainly, oil company investment plans are already underway in all the Middle Eastern countries and India. Banking capital and industrial capital are combining on a world scale to undertake oil exploration, refining and product development activities in the entire area.

The second option for allaying discontent is to expand war industries and other forms of public expenditures. Despite the balanced budget ideology of the Nixon administration, its efforts to maintain relatively high employment levels were concentrated on increasing defense contracts with large corporations and retaining the traditional Republican backing for highway and other transportation projects such as the expansion of the interstate highway program and pipeline construction to aid the flow of oil. A Democratic administration would certainly accelerate the volume of public spending to alleviate the economic crunch. The emergence of the "hawk" forces to a position of hegemony under Senator Henry M. Jackson ( D—Washington ) after the defeat of the liberal "doves" within the party prefigures the probability that the Democrats will run in the 1976 elections on a platform of guns and butter. The statement by Senator Jackson in spring 1974 that he would be willing to run for President on a ticket that included Alabama governor George Wallace may signal a realignment of the Democratic Party in a rightwing populist direction. The analogy to the alliance of the representative of eastern capital, Woodrow Wilson, with the leader of southern and western populism, William Jennings Bryan is uncanny. Wilson and Bryan combined a high degree of isolationism with a penchant for spouting the rhetoric of domestic reform. Jackson is a candidate with a long New Deal/Fair Deal record, fully supported by the AFL-CIO as well as the representatives of the pro-armament western capitalists. Wallace speaks for the anti-corporate, isolationist wing of the party, with a base among rank-and-file workers and agrarians. Neither is considered part of the statist, internationalist wing of the party that has held the reins of control since the 1930s. Yet, both are considered militant fighters against the growing domination of big business and big government over American life.

The new group within the Democratic Party would undoubtedly retain the populist aura that has marked the career of Governor Wallace. Senator Jackson demonstrated talent for trust busting in his championing of the interests of the independent refiners and marketers during the Senate hearings of April 1973. At the same time, he retains a strong identification with the military preparedness wing of the Senate, a good posture in times of economic crisis. The liberal wing will be hard pressed to hold back the bid of this powerful coalition, especially if the Jackson-Wallace candidacy is able to retain a commitment to welfare while, at the same time, expressing the anti-statist sentiments of its constituency. McGovern's defeat in 1972 is bound to hurt the chances of any candidate who poses as the logical heir of his program.

There can be no doubt that the military has influence in both parties especially in the wake of the almost unanimous congressional approval for the 8 billion dollar arms hike in 1974. The worsening economic situation within the U.S. will probably result in the widening of military influence. There are substantial problems in implementing this option. First, the United States lacks an available external enemy. Since the détentist policies of the Soviet

Union, and the emerging rapprochement between the United States and China have occurred, the old standby arguments for military preparedness have not been destroyed but they have certainly suffered erosion. Moreover, unless an enemy can be found, the heavier tax bite on the American people to pay for a steep rise in defense spending would encounter substantial political opposition. Second, the outcome of the Vietnam war has certainly dampened popular enthusiasm for military action. ·The most devastating feature of the Southeast Asia adventure was the deep understanding by most Americans that the doctrine of United States invincibility was a myth. In any case, short of the employment of nuclear weapons as an instrument of battle, there seems no chance of victory in a "limited war" against a determined popular enemy even if technical superiority can be maintained by the United States throughout.

Of course, there is always Europe and Japan. If these powers had managed to consolidate their independent economic position, or had challenged United States hegemony in the Middle East, the chances of war would have been greater. But the United States intervention into Southeast Asia appears to have thwarted Japanese ambitions in that area, except under the careful supervision of United States corporations. European powers never made a serious attempt to share influence with United States-based multinationals in the Middle East. Instead, European capital, particularly British and French investors, have accepted the direction of the United States corporations there. As I have argued, the independence of Europe was seriously shaken by the oil and food crises and the chances of recovery have become slimmer than ever before.

Which raises the distinct probability of the emergence of new forms of authoritarian rule at home. The pervasive enemy can no longer be located in the rhetoric of the "red peril" or the "yellow peril." The prospects for a war psychosis cannot be precluded if the détente fails. Yet, it is more likely, at least in the near future, that the preponderance of efforts by government and the corporations will be directed toward the elimination of internal sources of opposition.

The most important of these is crushing worker militancy. The propensity of employers to take advantage of adverse economic conditions by demanding increased productivity through speedup and stretchout will certainly encounter working class opposition. The crucial steps now being undertaken by the steel industry to deprive the workers of their strike weapon through voluntary agreement for the arbitration of all disputes including wage disputes is probably going to become the major corporate strategy in the next few years. There is no reason to believe that union leaders are hostile to the deferment of the strike weapon in favor of some important benefits to older members. However, some industries may not be in an economic position to offer sufficient incentives to get such an agreement. Among the options that cannot be precluded is that laws may be proposed to outlaw strikes under certain circumstances if collective bargaining fails. The disruption of production caused by strikes, particularly those directed against rising living costs, will certainly take on a political coloration in the future. Since the government and the largest corporations are closely intertwined, the development of a definite national incomes policy in the light of the current situation is more probable than ever. The incomes policy may be directed toward preventing workers from maintaining real wages, much less improving them. Thus, working class resistance to such measures will parallel the impact of the use of the strike weapon in Great Britain, where the miners' strike was able to bring down the Conservative government. The shaky United States national government can ill afford such strikes. Therefore, there is every reason to believe that the restriction of the strike weapon will become a major instrument of national policy.

There is mounting evidence of a more repressive corporate policy at the work place as well. The careful, systematic weeding out of militants in the auto industry is not confined to organized radicals. Wildcat strikes are being met by summary discharges in the auto industry. This was particularly evident in the 1973 walkout in the Chrysler stamping plant in Detroit, the discharge of the leader of black militants in the Ford Mahwah, New Jersey, plant and more than 40 workers in the Linden, New Jersey, plant of the General Motors Corporation. In all cases, the corporations were given assistance by the United Auto Workers. Similar collusion to crush discontent within the steel, telephone and trucking industries was in evidence during 1973 and 1974. Within the Teamsters Union, for example, the repression spread beyond the shop to include dissenting union officials. The forced retirement of Harold Gibbons, a leading liberal with the union and a vice president for many years, and the government indictments against several well-known local officials who supported George McGovern in 1972 and have maintained their autonomy from the growing centralized power of the national union, were signs that the labor movement was an important target of both the government and the labor bureaucracy.

I have already taken account of the decline of radical influence in the universities, but it must be noted that the enlargement of the repressive apparatus has extended to the teachers' unions as well. The 1974 Montreal convention of the American Federation of Teachers was among the most brilliant examples of machine consolidation in

the history of American trade unionism. Once a highly decentralized and relatively democratic organization, the
Teachers have been transformed into a highly centralized,
command organization modeled on military practice. The
new national president, Albert Shanker, represents a new
breed of trade union official, particularly among the more
chaotic public sector unions. He is not only aiming to
build an empire within the school industry, but seeks to
become George Meany's successor as president of
AFL-CIO. On the way, he has created a dynasty that fits
perfectly into the needs of the government in the public
sector. The past decade has witnessed the dramatic rise of
public employee unionism. Against the law, public employees have used the strike weapon with good effect,
having succeeded in raising wages, benefits and improving working conditions with swiftness and dispatch that
have become the envy of the older industrial and craft
organizations. The costs that have been incurred by this
activity have been reflected in high taxes at all levels of
government. The election of Shanker suggests the possibility of more strict enforcement of the strike ban, a centralized mechanism for bargaining, and a more strictly
disciplined labor force in this sector. Shanker is shrewd,
conservative in politics and highly single-minded. In
short, he is a perfect union leader for the new economic
and political situation. If he is successful in preventing
the tide of protest and dissent that brought him to power
in the 1960s from continuing into the next decade, he will
be a perfect candidate for the role of labor statesman, and
earn the gratitude of corporate America.

We are on the road to what Bertram Gross has called
"friendly fascism."[1] Unlike its European predecessors,
American fascism may not be marked by an "open terror-
istic dictatorship." The foundation of fascism has already
been laid in the consolidation of political and economic

power in incredibly few hands. The strengthening of the executive branch of government to the point of almost dictatorial power has taken place without the traditional symbols of repression. No synagogues have been smashed, radical and workers' organizations remain legally operating, and there has been no mass roundup of the Left. Yet, Congress and other legislative bodies have already been effectively preempted of their prerogatives both by law and by custom. The distinctions between executive, legislative and corporate spheres have been blurred if not completely obliterated. Under these conditions, there is absolutely no reason to dissolve the Congress. Moreover, trade unions can continue to operate as long as they are useful for the implementation of national policy—as long as they assist in the task of disciplining the labor force. The vocationalization of education and the concomitant decline of the liberal arts and humanities are other features of the gentle repression.

These tendencies are maturing rapidly. The highly publicized secret study by the RAND Corporation prior to the last Presidential election setting forth the conditions under which a national election may be suspended will probably not have to be implemented as long as the Democratic Party, its working class and middle class constituencies, remain in disarray. Democratic forms are always a more effective method of rule as long as the scale of opposition remains sporadic and uncoordinated. Countervailing the judgment that fascism is arriving without terror is the possible consequence of the crisis of legitimacy. Under these circumstances, resistance may turn into rebellion since the corporate capitalist class lacks the symbols needed to maintain a high degree of trust in its rule. Pluralism as an ideology has declined in proportion to its eclipse in practice. Only the most authoritarian new ideologies such as those which invest wisdom and power in the hands of a single leader may be adequate to the new corporate priorities.

Such a leader would have to attach himself to the coat-tails of protest and resistance. The material conditions exist for such a development since the requirement of aus-terity has no recent legitimation outside of war prepara-tions.

On the other side, the real basis exists for the new radicalism as well. Against the power of central bureauc-racies in government and the corporations, the demand for popular control of social and economic institutions and a socialist alternative to the hortatory direction of na-tional life has greater resonance, at least incipiently, among the population. The question of revolutionary poli-tics is no longer to be regarded as rhetorical, but may be seen as a practical chance to overcome the long-term movement toward regimentation, military discipline in the work place and in the neighborhood and the ultimate danger of war as the only resolution of the crisis.

Resistance to the authoritarian tendencies inherent in the food and energy crises cannot be confined to propos-als for the restoration of the balance of government power in the direction of greater legislative autonomy and con-trol, although this step is certainly desirable. Nor would government ownership of energy industries contribute significantly to stemming the assault on living standards as long as the government itself remains structurally tied to the corporate economy. A cursory glance at the expe-rience of government ownership of utilities and basic in-dustries in Western Europe leaves little room for opti-mism, especially for workers employed in these enterprises who often face even more severe curbs when they strike or undertake other protest activities.

Certainly the history of government regulation of big industry in the past seventy-five years within the United

States reveals that it has consistently operated in the interest of the regulated rather than the public. The greatest beneficiaries of the controls of the last several years were the corporations themselves. Government antitrust policies have never been directed against the most powerful corporations, except in token measures. In the main, antitrust has been a weapon of the largest corporations against the upstarts. The use of government regulation to foster economic concentration rather than competition has been far more significant than its trust busting activities under both Republican and Democratic administrations.

The real alternatives are to be found, not in strengthening central government administration of the economy, but in a radically new technology and mode of social control. On one hand, new forms of energy can be developed to replace the regressive coal and oil industries. The solar, geothermal and fusion sources of energy do not rely on fossils, would not require the devastation of the physical environment and would not be limited in their quantities. To be sure, some of the technologies for the use of such sources are "uneconomical" in relation to the ratio of capital investment to profit, and research is still at a relatively low level, particularly in terms of the practical issues involved. But it is plain that government policy is now directed toward finding new sources of coal and oil rather than using tax money for research in new fields. This is a political, not a technical, question.

On the other hand, the new energy sources would permit new modes of management. Public power need not imply government monopoly. Instead it could be managed by workers and consumers on a local level, and central resources could be confined to research and coordination. Solar, windmill and fusion power, by their very nature, lend themselves to decentralized systems of coordination and administration. The international economy is created, in part, by the technologies employed and these technologies, now a fait accompli, thus seem perfectly "natural." Breaking the power of the oil industry over energy and the dependence of whole populations on the vicissitudes of international oil politics requires, not only the nationalization of oil, but its eventual replacement. At the very least, changing power relations within the energy industries would require a plurality of choices for meeting the needs of industrial production and public utilities.

The notion of private ownership of utilities is a peculiarly American aberration. The scandalous performance of such giant power companies as ConEdison and Public Service Gas & Electric in New York and New Jersey respectively disproves the dictum that private enterprise is inherently more efficient than public ownership. The constant specter of summer "brownouts" makes both agencies poor risks for the maintenance of essential services. Thus the argument for worker and consumer management is no longer a moral invocation. It has become at least as practical an option as the present arrangement.

The movement for new social arrangements presupposes more than an articulate political opposition. In fact it may be argued that a genuine radical alternative to the global policies of the supranationals cannot be generated without a new sense of self-awareness among the population.

The central ingredient of this self awareness is already apparent in the impulse away from the wanton consumption of social waste, the subversive character of the end of patriotism, and the incipient efforts of young Americans to redefine their priorities. The creation of countercultural communities in the late 1960s was a form of political opposition to the material foundations of the United States corporate system to the extent that it represented a rejection of atomistic ways of life. But this counterculture was successfully isolated from the mainstream of American politics and culture and failed to penetrate the consciousness of most Americans.

It remains imperative that we examine how the giant corporations were able to impose their priorities on the whole country without encountering effective opposition. The main point of this book has been to argue that the explanation of events of the past two years cannot be confined to the categories of administrative and political manipulation, or repression by force, although these have been marked features of the energy and food coups that were successfully completed in 1972-73.

The capacity of the United States to avoid the most repressive forms of rule available to human beings in wartime and economic crisis was always predicated on the privileged position enjoyed by this country in terms of standard of living, productive expansion and being spared from physical destruction. These presuppositions no longer obtain. And herein lies the danger. The advances in military technology make United States destruction as probable in the event of another war as that of any other country. The decline of the United States *national* economy has raised the question of whether the erosion of all democratic forms in this country can be justified in terms of economic superiority over others. This is the real choice now before Americans: *shall we, on the basis of our internalized sense of helplessness to deal with global issues, accept the game plan of the large corporations and its unintended consequences, or shall the means be found to offer more than resistance, that is, concerted efforts to overcome the crisis on the basis of a broad, democratic movement for the transfer of management over our economy and social life?*

# Acknowledgments

The five chapters comprising this volume are essentially analytic and speculative. Much of the research has been culled from daily newspaper reports, government documents and personal sources. Individuals working for news media and oil companies have helped enormously in providing material. Unfortunately, some of them cannot be named, although the public sources are documented.

A special thanks must go to the Union of Radical Political Economists, whose work on food ranks as a fine example of committed, dispassionate research and analysis. Michael Roloff and Margot Shields of Seabury Press were incredibly patient with me and a source of constant assistance throughout. I have learned much from several conversations with Robert Lekachman, David Nasaw and Arlo Fischer on topics covered in this book. Of course, none of the persons from whom I have learned much, bear any responsibility for its errors.

S. A.

# Notes

### 1. CONTOURS OF A TROUBLED SOCIETY

1. Donald D. Durost and Glen T. Barton, "Changing Sources of Farm Output," USDA Agricultural Research Service, *Production Research Report* #36, February 1960, pp. 9-13.

2. *Ibid.*

3. Broadus Mitchell, *Depression Decade: From New Era Through New Deal, 1929–1941.* New York: Holt, Rinehart & Winston, 1947.

4. 1969 Census of Agriculture.

5. The term is the title of a book by Theodor W. Adorno, published by Northwestern University Press in 1973. In the context of this chapter it means something different from the critique of Heidegger. I employ the term to connote the feverish search for the elusive self that has been produced by consumerism as a way of life.

6. F. S. Perls, *Ego, Hunger and Aggression.* New York: Random House, 1969.

## 2. BUTTER FROM BOEING, HAM FROM ITT

1. *Economic Indicators.* Published by the Joint Economic Committee, United States Congress, October 1973.

2. *Business Week,* April 28, 1973.

3. Edward Higbee, *Farms and Farmers in an Urban Age.* Twentieth Century Fund, 1963, p. 9.

4. William Appleman Williams, *The Roots of Modern American Empire.* New York: Random House, 1969.

5. Lloyd Gardner, *Economic Aspects of New Deal Diplomacy.* Madison: University of Wisconsin Press, 1964.

6. Higbee, op. cit.

7. Higbee, op. cit., chapter one.

8. 1969 Census of Agriculture; *Fortune,* July 1973, p. 112; *Who Will Control U.S. Agriculture?* Agricultural Extension Services, University of Illinois at Champaigne-Urbana, August 1972.

9. Higbee, op. cit., p. 8.

10. Higbee, op. cit., p. 14.

11. *Employment and Earnings,* U.S. Department of Labor, Vol. 3, September 1973 (23).

12. *Ibid.*

13. Ben Seligman, *Economics of Dissent.* Chicago: Quadrangle, 1968.

14. Erich Fromm, *Escape from Freedom.* New York: Avon, 1968, chapter four.

15. This table was compiled by Carol Lopate, on the basis of first-hand observations of supermarkets in the New York City area in February 1974. Although prices outside of New York may be significantly lower, variations will occur proportionally.

## 3. "SEVEN SISTERS" ON THE MAKE

1. Thomas Bradshaw.

2. *Wall Street Journal,* January 28, 1974.

3. Michael Tanzer, *The Political Economy of International Oil and the Underdeveloped Countries.* Boston: Beacon Press, 1969, chapter two. Tanzer's calculations conflict, in some respects, with those of other informed oil analysts. For example, his estimate of the cost of production for Venezuelan crude is 20 cents lower than

others such as M. A. Edelman, and OPEC data. The main point obtains in both estimates: the cost of crude oil production, from which most oil company profits have been hitherto extracted, is extremely low. The major international oil monopolies have been able to share profits with the OPEC countries precisely because of these low costs.

4. Transportation costs from the Middle East are no more than 20% of a barrel of crude oil. The oil companies which were earning 88 cents on a barrel of crude oil between 1960–65, increased their volume of profit from $1.04 to $1.10 by June 1973, just as the "crisis" was beginning to break. By January 1974 a barrel of crude oil brought $4.46 profit after a tax of $7.00 imposed by the oil-producing countries of the Middle East. (*Business Week,* February 2, 1974)

5. Robert G. Dunlop, Sun Oil Company president and chairman American Petroleum Institute, addressing the Institute's Annual Meeting in Chicago, November 15, 1967. (CPA Editorial Services, July 3, 1973)

6. Statement of H. Donald Borger, chairman and chief executive officer Consolidated Natural Gas Company, and chairman of the government relations committee, American Gas Association, before House Ways and Means Committee, March 21, 1969. (CPA Editorial Services)

7. Robert G. Dunlop, president Sun Oil Company, before Subcommittee on Antitrust and Monopoly of the Senate Judiciary Committee, May 22, 1969. (CPA Editorial Services)

### 4. CONSEQUENCES OF THE CRISES

1. Declining enrollment in the social sciences and humanities in graduate schools threatens the need to provide ideologists for the corporate system who will perform teaching, research and writing functions. With the exception of anthropology, such fields as philosophy, sociology and especially history have suffered from the exodus of young scholars. This problem only finds its immediate cause in the closing of the job market in colleges and universities and secondary schools. More long-range reasons for the end of the social sciences within the universities, except at the undergraduate level where they are given as required courses, are the end of hope

among students that the fruits of scholarship can be linked to social reform.

2. *Business Week*, April 13, 1974.

## 5. THE FUTURE OF THE AMERICAN DREAM

1. Bertram Gross, "Friendly Fascism" in *Social Policy*, November-December 1970.

# Selected Bibliography

ON FOOD AND AGRICULTURE

Allan G. Bogue, *From Prairie to Cornbelt: Farming on the Illinois and Ohio Prairie in the 19th Century*. Chicago: Quadrangle, 1968.

Karl A. Fox, Vernon W. Ruttan and Lawrence W. Witt, *Farming, Farmers and Markets for Farm Goods: Essays on the Problems of American Agriculture*, Supplementary Paper No. 15, New York Committee for Economic Development, 1962.

Edward Higbee, *Farms and Farmers in an Urban Age*. New York: Twentieth Century Fund, 1963.

Broadus Mitchell, *Depression Decade: From New Era through New Deal 1929-1941*. New York: Holt, Rinehart & Winston, 1947.

William Robbins, *The American Food Scandal*. New York: William Morrow, 1974.

Ben Seligman, *Economics of Dissent*. Chicago: Quadrangle, 1968, "The High Cost of Eating."

Alvin S. Tostlebe, *The Growth of Physical Capital in Agriculture 1870–1950*, Occasional Paper 44, National Bureau of Economic Research, 1954.

William Appleman Williams, *Roots of Modern American Empire*. New York: Random House, 1969.

## ON OIL AND OTHER ENERGY RESOURCES

Robert Engler, *The Politics of Oil*. New York: Macmillan, 1961.
Rob Dumont and John W. Warnock, "The ABCs of Oil," *Canadian Dimension*, Vol. 7, nos. 7, 8, no date.
James F. Gannon, "Too Big a Price?" *Wall Street Journal*, March 6, 1974.
Carol J. Loomis, "How to Think About Oil Company Profits," *Fortune*, April 1974.
*Report of Senate Committee on Government Operations*, April 1973.
Sanford Rose, "The Far Reaching Consequences of High-Priced Oil," *Fortune*, April 1974.
Michael Tanzer, *The Political Economy of International Oil and Underdeveloped Countries*. Boston: Beacon Press, 1969.
"The New Shape of the Oil Industry," *Business Week*, February 2, 1974.
United States Tariff Commission, *World Oil Development and U.S. Oil Import Policies*, TC Publication 632, Washington, D.C., October 1973.

## GENERAL

Stanley Aronowitz, *False Promises*. New York: McGraw-Hill, 1973.
Shlomo Avineri, *Hegel's Theory of the Modern State*. New York: Oxford University Press, 1972.
John M. Blair, *Economic Concentration: Structure, Behavior and Public Policy*. New York: Harcourt, Brace Jovanovich, 1972.
Max Horkheimer and Theodor Adorno, *Dialectic of the Enlightenment*, New York: Herder and Herder, 1972.
M. Hudson, *Super Imperialism: The Economic Strategy of the American Empire*. New York: Holt, Rhinehart & Winston, 1971.
V. I. Lenin, *Imperialism: The Highest Stage of Capitalism*. New York: International Publishers, 1943.
Harry Magdoff, *The Age of Imperialism*. New York: Monthly Review Press, 1969.
James O'Connor, *The Fiscal Crisis of the State*. New York: St. Martin's Press, 1973.

Maurice Merleau Ponty, *Adventures of the Dialectic*. Evanston: Northwestern University Press, 1973.

William Serrin, *The Company and the Union*, New York: Knopf, 1973.

Herbert Stein, *The Fiscal Revolution in America*. Chicago: University of Chicago Press, 1969.

# Index

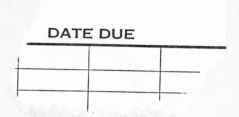

DATE DUE